Living Gaudí

First published in the United States of America in 2002 by
Rizzoli International Publications, Inc.
300 Park Avenue South
New York, NY 10010
www.rizzoliusa.com

Originally published in Spanish in 2001 as *Gaudí: Hábitat, Naturaleza y Cosmos* by
Lunwerg Editores, Barcelona

© International Rights
   Lunwerg Editores, Barcelona, 2002
   Editoriale Jaca Book Spa, Milán, 2002

© For the texts: Maria Antonietta Crippa, Joan Bassegoda Nonell, Francesc Navés Viñas, Joan Morell Núñez

© Photography: Marc LLimargas

Design by Lunwerg Editores, with the help of La Mirada Sonora

Copyright © 2002 Rizzoli International Publications, Inc., for English edition
Second printing 2006
2006 2007 2008 2009 / 10 9 8 7 6 5 4 3 2

Printed and bound in Spain

Library of Congress Control Number: 2001099075
ISBN-10: 0-8478-2435-7
ISBN-13: 978-0-8478-2435-9

Living Gaudí

THE ARCHITECT'S COMPLETE VISION

Edited by

MARIA ANTONIETTA CRIPPA

Photography by

MARC LLIMARGAS

Text by

JOAN BASSEGODA NONELL
MARIA ANTONIETTA CRIPPA
JOAN MORELL NÚÑEZ
FRANCESC NAVÉS VIÑAS

Rizzoli
NEW YORK

CONTENTS

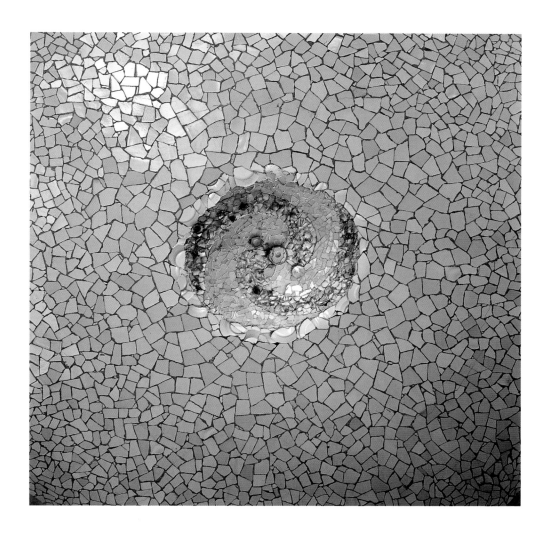

A DWELLING FOR MAN WITHIN
THE HARMONY OF THE COSMOS

Maria Antonietta Crippa

Stone column on the second floor of Casa Milá with inscriptions in relief. The structure is composed solely of columns, without any other walls than those of the façade, which contains large windows that look out onto Paseo de Grácia.

T HIS BOOK PRESENTS A UNIFIED INTERPRETATION OF ANTONIO GAUDÍ'S approach to house construction, an area in which he made a contribution to contemporary architecture that extended far beyond western boundaries, a contribution of exceptional originality and one that is still packed with prophetic indicators. The critical slant of the book places house design in close relation to the planning of parks and gardens, since the artificial world of architecture was continuously interacting with nature, both in Gaudí's imagination and in his actual designs. In addition, this interplay between the built and natural worlds represents an interesting response to ecological demands that have in recent years become impossible to ignore.

In fact, Gaudí's approach to house design derives not only from the reciprocal dialogue he creates between constructive artifice and the natural elements of landscaping, but also from the

The courtyard of Casa Milá on the Calle Provença side. The stairway leads up to the main apartment, which is the Milá-Segimon residence. The plinth, shaft, and capital of the columns are made of rustic wood, while among the columns there are ostentatious jardinières which hold trailing plants.

masterly way in which he assimilates and transfigures the natural elements into architectural components within the actual creative process of construction. This second point was an approach that he developed by creating constructive and figurative elements that were unprecedented in the history of architecture. Consider, for example, the way that he uses catenary structures and fluted surfaces, or the features that appear in his artificial landscapes and stone gardens; these elements all work to create a fantasy world, as in the case of the multitextured, undulating façade of Casa Batlló, or the mysterious ghost world on the roof terrace of Casa Milá.

Gaudí's houses and gardens are evidently a synthesis of his sharp observation of natural phenomena, his constructional intelligence, and his fervent imagination, as well as multilayered symbolic allusions. But above all, they express the explosive advent of a cosmic energy in the

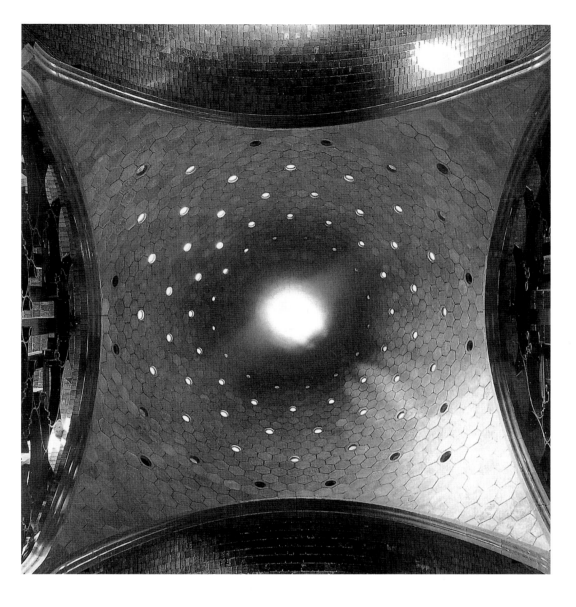

Dome above the main living room at Palacio Güell. Comprised of baída vaulting on catenary arches and a full paraboloidal profile. It has a perforated keystone and several concentric circular holes which let in light from the exterior. This section is in turn covered by a conical structure, which is also perforated to allow light to enter. The intrados is tiled with hexagonal ceramic pieces.

Catalan architect's creative talent, an energy that succeeds in blending matter and spirit, mankind and objects, architecture and nature. The prophetic nature of this creative force can be recognized today, yet for most of Gaudí's contemporaries—both architects and critics—it seemed to go against the flow of history.

His constructions were built at the time when a utopian, secularizing trend was developing in the world of European architecture. This trend, which was radically different from the direction taken by the Catalan architect, proposed the creation of new urban and residential spaces that would resolve the imbalances caused by the violent growth of cities and by the technological revolution that took place in the second half of the nineteenth century and the beginning of the twentieth.

Historical Context

In order to appreciate Gaudí's originality, we must first look at the context in which he worked. During the late nineteenth and early twentieth centuries, architecture was changing from a style in which eclecticism coexisted with an engineering-based architecture to the first and most explosive expression of a Modernism that was eminently rational (if one excludes the dazzling period of German expressionism, which had little effect on house design). The basic aspects of this rationality were developed during the 1920s and '30s. Early in the twentieth century,

Interior of the main apartment at Casa Milá during the remodeling project in 1968. Note the bare structure, the stone pillars, the iron main beams, metal girders, and brick vaulting. Beneath the wrought iron there used to be three-dimensional plaster ceilings that Señora Milá ordered to be removed in 1926.

between the two world wars, the Art Nouveau school appeared. It started in Belgium, and immediately spread across Europe. The ornamental approach of Art Nouveau—which was sometimes floral in style, other times more geometric—was given a variety of names (such as Modernism, Modern style, "flowery" style, Liberty, and Sezession) in the countries where it developed.

The effects of illuminist culture and of the industrial and urban revolutions had by then been fully consolidated, and all contributed to a radical transformation in the area of anthropology—both urban and rural—and in the terms employed by engineers and architects. Above all, two factors had emerged at the end of the nineteenth century which would act as catalysts for significant change. First, technological innovations facilitated the rapid diffusion of buildings in iron and reinforced concrete, as well as an increase in domestic comforts produced by the supply of electricity, water, and gas to people's homes. Second, the rapid spread of new approaches to urban settlement immediately created a need for regulatory control in town planning. This in turn led to the creation of two different types of residential buildings: the chalet-villa with its own garden, which would become the detached residence (generally situated in the suburbs) of the nuclear family, and the multidwelling tenement house, for which architects have produced many different designs, typologically distinguishing between the middle-class urban residential block and the working-class multiapartment house.

Aerial view of the Sagrada Familia Provisional Schools (1909). The brick vaulting roof has the geometric shape of two guiding plane conoids which share a straight generatrix in the axis of the building, beneath which is situated the only iron main beam in the structure.

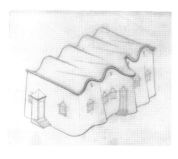

Drawing of the Sagrada Familia Provisional Schools together with the hyperbolic paraboloid walls and the conoidal roof. The small building on the right contains the toilets.

Between 1890 and 1914, construction became increasingly focused on these areas, fostering a mentality that was proto-rationalist, anti-monumental, and tending toward simplification. This approach was first adopted by builders, only to be immediately taken on board by architects, who were gradually becoming conscious of the limitations of their academic training.

There was also a growing interest in industrial processes that could be used in construction, while the increasingly urgent demand for comfort and technological innovation resulted in a decline in lavish ornamentation and stylistic refinement in the decorative pieces that European craftsmen had been producing for centuries.

All these transformations did not occur gradually; they came about as a result of a series of rapid, violent changes in direction, fluctuations in taste, and ideological conflicts. In the opening decades of the twentieth century, all this led to (among other things) a coexistence, in many areas, between a belated eclecticism, Art Nouveau, and proto-rationalism. This coexistence possessed its own distinctive national flavor from country to country, but designers were following a single cultural trend that had spread across the entire western world. Meanwhile, it had become necessary to define new urban development programs, both as a result of the ever-increasing demand for working-class housing and as a result of the advent of national reformist movements that advocated the use of new technological resources for the purpose of providing the greatest good to the greatest possible number of people.

From 1880 on (and within a social and political context strongly influenced by socialist and Marxist thought), many organizations that had appeared in Europe advocated collaboration and the exchange of ideas between artists, craftsmen, and owners of industrial firms connected with the sphere of construction. The aim was to foment an industry that could compete quali-

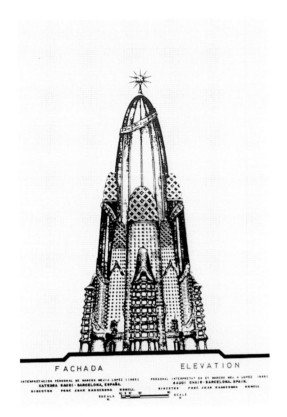

FACHADA   ELEVATION

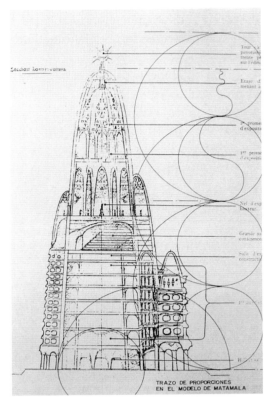

TRAZO DE PROPORCIONES
EN EL MODELO DE MATAMALA

A study of the elevation of the project for the Hotel Attraction in New York, implemented in 1995 by the architect Marcos Mejia Lopez from original sketches by Gaudí (1908) and drawings by Juan Matamala Flotats (1965).

A study of the proportions of the Hotel Attraction in New York, by Marcos Mejía Lopez, who was awarded his doctorate in architecture by the Catedra Gaudí in September 1995. He also designed an exhibition that opened at the Rey Juan Carlos I Hotel in Barcelona, on December 21, 1993 and made a film for Catalonia Television, for the program *Stromboli*.

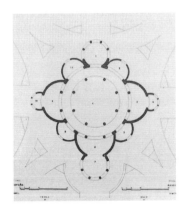

Schematic ground plan of the Hotel Attraction in New York, based on works by Juan Matamala which were published in 1989 in *The Great Gaudí* and on studies by Marcos Mejía Lopez.

tatively with traditional arts and handicrafts in the production of constructional and decorative elements. The most famous groups of this kind were the English Arts and Crafts movement of the late eighteenth century, the Austrian Wiener Werkstätte (founded in 1903), and the Deutscher Werkbund (1907) of Germany.

In the U.S., rapid industrial development led to the invention of the metal-frame sky-scraper around 1870, which was used mainly for offices. However, the use of metal frames for smaller buildings in the U.S. also rivaled traditional brickwork-and-stone building methods (and this occurred much earlier than in Europe). As an immediate result, there were great developments in the area of building support, as well as work on the prefabrication of components and their industrial production. By the end of the nineteenth century, both in Europe and in America, large structures were being built in iron and glass. This period saw the advent of the electrical elevator, as well as central heating, air conditioning, lighting units, and emergency antifire systems in offices. It was electricity, above all, that facilitated the growing mechanization of such facilities within the home, unleashing an even greater demand for home comforts.

The new approach to building was dominated by the typology of the skeletal structure, which replaced the traditional structure based on load-bearing walls. The new system was also faster to build, and therefore it became possible to reduce the time that invested capital, which usually came from private enterprise and companies, was tied up in such projects. Reinforced concrete was introduced after iron and was first used above all in Europe. At the beginning of the twentieth century, the Perret brothers in Paris and Heilmann and Litmann in Munich constructed buildings with exposed reinforced-concrete structures, paving the way for a new aesthetic which the pioneers of manufacturing processes would soon merge with their own speculation-based interests. In America, reinforced concrete was first used mainly for silos and tanks; it only became widely used in civil construction after the earthquake of 1906.

During these years, engineers achieved significant aesthetic results in the design of land-based infrastructures or large building complexes, thanks to a refined search for disciplined rationality taken from the field of building and applied to new materials. Consider, for example, the elegant bridges in reinforced concrete built by Maillard, or huge complexes such as the reinforced-concrete dome of Jahrhunderthalle, built by Max Berg in Breslau in 1913 (now Wroclaw, Poland).

The rapid industrialization of construction in certain countries led to the use of new nonflammable materials, such as asbestos and asbestos cement. Ice-resistant enameled ceramics were manufactured for use as wall surfaces; the linoleum floor was invented; and the market was flooded with industrially manufactured blown glass, making it possible to create even larger windows. One result of all these advances was a considerable increase in house prices.

Though in the West it had become the most important area of planning, the new dwelling—whether it was a detached house or a group of different homes—was not developed through a linear process. While, for example, elevations—above all, the street façades—continued for a long time to include eclectic or Art Nouveau features in many European cities, the new systems of internal functional organization were quickly introduced everywhere.

In the historicist nineteenth century, the internationalization of the house brought about a realization of the scale on which the landscape was rapidly losing its identity, at both a local and a regional level. Perhaps Viollet-le-Duc was the first to compare different ways of life in civilizations on very different latitudes.

The consequences of the uncontrolled growth that took place in many western cities—such as Chicago, New York, Paris, Berlin, Vienna, and Barcelona—also provoked a widespread antiurban reaction, a rejection of the living conditions imposed by the metropolis. This subject was popular with those who were evoking socialist utopias of the nineteenth century, but it persisted during a large part of the following century in the form of Ebenezer Howard's model (repeated and reinterpreted several times) of the Garden City, which stimulated the collective imagination with its dream of synthesizing the best elements of the city and the country into one single way of life.

At the same time, from the second half of the nineteenth century on, the great western cities saw a sharp increase in the construction of buildings for public use, which were sometimes gigantic in scale and monumental in appearance (large department stores, railway stations, theaters, and parks), all within the framework of modernization processes. In Europe, the reference models included the rapid transformation of Paris (strictly supervised by Baron Haussmann, who was implementing the wishes of Napoleon III) and the construction of the Vienna Ring, a project that showed greater respect for the city's historical fabric.

In general, from 1890 on the question of house design became central to the field of architecture. Architects studied the difference in forms between the detached house and the multidwelling construction, thus laying the foundations for research (in the areas of architecture and town planning) which in the 1920s and '30s would represent the main focus for the best architects who were doing pioneering work into new forms of human settlement.

The frantic division of land into lots, the growing inequality in the cost of renting urban land, and the rise in speculation all served to encourage the middle classes to move out to suburban chalet-villas, where they duly demanded the immediate application of all the typological innovations. In most cases, the buildings under construction in the city were inevitably adapted to these building typologies—the shape of the lot, a controlled containment of volumes, and an appreciation of gardens (always limited in size, for the enjoyment of which terraces, more windows, balconies, and secondary accesses were added). Comfort, functionality, and economy of consumption became key elements in these plans, by imposing onto the building processes a rigorous rationalization as well as new opportunities.

The logical result and main consequence of these developments was the general discarding of planimetric organization. Façade designs, especially streetside façades, were characterized by asymmetrical patterns and openly prominent sections, thereby signaling a rejection of representational designs on the façades. At the same time, representational sections in the house's interior were reduced to a minimum, stripping away redundant

Imaginary view of one of the dining rooms in the Hotel Attraction in New York, in a drawing by Juan Matamala Flotats, who inherited some of Gaudí's original sketches from his father, and who knew (from the family's oral tradition) the general form of the building of which Gaudí had only made sketches.

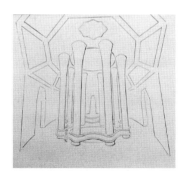

Central support colonnade for the large upper lounge in the Hotel Attraction in New York, by Juan Matamala. It is reminiscent of the form of the support for the dome at the Sagrada Familia which Gaudí demonstrated in scale models made of plaster.

Arbor, on the corner of Calle Sant Gervasi (now Calle de las Carolinas) and the Callejón de Sant Gervasi in the garden of Casa Vicens. This arrangement disappeared in the reformation in 1927. The exposed brick entablature stood on short stone columns.

eighteenth-century ostentation. Very gradually, a real revolution in everyday life began, one in which the relationship between the client and the architect was of great importance. Soon, magazines on art and interior decoration began to appear, and through such publications a great many people became familiar with the Art Nouveau house, the proto-rationalist house, and the organic house.

In the nineteenth and early twentieth centuries, a series of laws was passed which fomented and financially supported the creation of working-class neighborhoods. Such projects involved the urban organization of extensive areas (and also, therefore, of infrastructures and public spaces) and became an increasingly attractive proposition for famous architects, who carried out experiments in this field in search of the *existenz minimum*, the economic rationality of the building process and its aesthetic possibilities.

After World War I, ideas began to circulate more and more quickly and systematically until a perception of unity of experience and innovation was established on an international scale. At the beginning of the 1920s, Adolf Behne and Walter Gropius were championing a fully matured, international Modern architecture. Their vision of the contemporary house was the result of a discrediting of historical and local traditions.

This trend, caught on quickly, causing architects to view their profession as separate from the need to serve specific social realities and respond to the symbolic density engraved in the history of a place. Instead they imagined the possibility of making innovations in housing

The gate of the Miralles building before the restoration in 2000. The metal canopy and the iron cross at the top are missing. Domingo Sugrañes took part in this project—the same architect who created the Valencia-style thatched house that can be seen in the garden.

Sketch by Domingo Sugrañes of the gate of the Miralles building, the now-disappeared Valencia-style thatched house, and the house that was never built.

First International Congress of Contemporary Architecture in La Sarraz (1928). Le Corbusier, Siegfried Giedion, García Mercadal, and other enthusiasts of rationalism.

design based on a theoretical interpretation of the needs of individuals with the result spreading uniformly throughout the civilized world. Thus the architect began to present himself as a leading figure in the sphere of social progress, a person who used his designs as the catalyst for a new democratic society. Though architects were very much aware of how difficult it would be to implement this proposition—surmounting problems of style in the name of the greater cause of social justice—they were also very excited, as they saw it as an imminent process, or even one that had already begun. To this end, the most famous western architects began to work together from 1928 on: They held international conferences on Modern architecture, and Le Corbusier was among those who played a fundamental role at these meetings.

Notre-Dame-du-Haut chapel in Ronchamp (1950–1955), a work by Le Corbusier in an organicist style—very different from his coolly rationalistic works of the thirties.

Embracing a double polarity, the Modern Movement was clearly characterized on one hand by a social function that was closely linked to technological advances, and on the other hand by its own original aesthetic approach (tied to aesthetics, imagination, and the compositional methods of the artistic avant-garde) which was based on a desire for strict coherence—and, ultimately, identification—between method and form.

Therefore, there was a desire to bring together, at least tangentially, the useful and the beautiful, and perhaps it was for this reason that rationalism led to a radical functionalism. Yet, (as a result of the work of the better-known architects, who immediately influenced architectural education), this new aesthetic sensitivity led to the creation of a language that was tangentially anti-ornamental but rich in subjective variations. In the early 1930s Henry-Russell Hitchcock, an American, would christen this language International Style.

Many architects (such as Le Corbusier, with his suggestive, stimulating approach to construction) managed to join the two trends without becoming mired in excessive schematization. Others, however, were perfect examples of either the first trend (Hannes Meyer) or the second (Mies van der Rohe). Thus the Modern building methods and figurative inventions of the artistic avant-garde were used for the purposes of a peaceful social revolution: Architectural design was transformed into a hypothesis to promote (and even provoke) the advent of the "new man" and a "new society." During these years, in the Russia which, following a bloody revolution, had become the Soviet Union, they rapidly progressed from the constructivists' avant-garde "machine" symbolism to a pompous, affected eclecticism established by bureaucracy and Stalinism.

This quick historical excursus that we have just made, an excursus that has focused more on the factual details of the great environmental transformations brought about during the last one hundred years or so than on the contemporary circulation of ideas, is merely an attempt to sketch out the basic process of transforming ways of living, from the city structure to the dwelling, and to establish a background against which we can consider Gaudí's work.

I have attempted to set out the reasons why many architects of the Modern Movement sought to reduce the house to a mechanism that was fitted with all manner of home comforts and that was based, like the contemporary idea of the city, on the development of a plan conceived solely as a rational response to a casuistry of the needs of the individual and of the society, and that was theoretically unlimited.

It is not my intention to criticize the process that I have just described. On the contrary, I think that it represents a heritage of disparate experiences that are still fundamental. In terms of weight and significance, the approaches put in for the same context by, for example, Bruno Taut, Martin Wagner, and Ernst May are all very different. Also of interest are their designs for rows of houses, three or four stories in height, with transverse apartments, often designed with private gardens. The residential prototypes by leading architects of the Modern Movement, which were shown in the 1927 Werkbund exhibition in Stüttgart (planned by Mies van de Rohe), are not archeological examples of a dated modernity. The Karl Marx Hof, comprising 1,600 dwellings arranged in the symbolic shape of a huge bastion and built on commission from the City Council of Vienna, still has its charm and cannot be judged solely by its ideological profile.

This list could go on and on: I could mention, for example, Hendrik Petrus Berlage's plan for a neighborhood in south Amsterdam (1917), or the stimulating design for a redbrick town, commissioned by the diamond workers' union and built by de Klerk in 1919–21, or the Kiefhoeck complex built by Oud and van Eesteren in 1925–27. With respect to France, I could cite the Plan Voisin (1925) by Le Corbusier, and the concept of the tenement dwelling that was promoted by a number of mayors in the *arrondissements* of Paris. When likened to these and many other examples of Modern dwellings, Gaudí's houses display a discontinuity and an overall diversity that is worth analyzing—without merely viewing them as two opposing approaches devoid of reciprocal influence. In my opinion, this breach may contain an important message for the near future. In order to examine it, we must avoid any kind of mythicization, condemnation, or any impossible (or at least inopportune) comparisons.

A Solitary (Though Not Individualistic) Search

In comparison with many of the abovementioned architects, Gaudí demonstrated an imaginative energy that was unique. In my opinion, this is the result of his discovery—during the course of a search that was completely solitary but not individualistic—of the holy dimension in its purest sense, in terms that become incomprehensible if one judges his images to be directly derived from Catholicism. Of course he was a Catholic of the extreme radical variety, and he explored the meaning of existence and history which led him to regain what we—along with Eliade, Dumézil, and Ries[1]—might call sacred or stratified religious meaning in the history of western culture but which, at the same time, was based entirely in Indo-European origins.

One could say that Gaudí used architecture to explore the mystery of life and its destiny by attempting to re-create, personally and with increasingly greater freedom (with respect both to long-fossilized stylistic canons and to the didactic ethics that he imagined), man's entire figurative heritage—both Oriental and European—recovering them through his memories, direct and indirect, and through photographic reproductions.

In Gaudí's work, the social dimension, metaphysical foundation, and specific expressiveness of holiness within a Christian framework are all blended together, unleashing a style of architecture that combines pre-Christian and Christian signs and symbols from both the East and the West, all in a completely new way. Using the organic nature of his architectural constructions, he also invented unprecedented allusive forms and figurative syntheses that reintroduced a primordial element of Indo-European culture into our consciousness, one that Eliade explained as: the idea that the act of building, of constructing, is something that has its very roots buried in cosmogonic myth, according to which the creation of a dwelling for people to live in is an act that implies "re-creating the World."

Let us consider, for example, Gaudí's need to establish some kind of orientation in space with those cosmic crosses that sprout from the tops of the most varied constructions and from the landscape itself. For the "primitive peoples," writes Eliade "the dividing of space into four horizons was equivalent to founding the World. The homogeneity of space, understood in a certain way, was associated with Chaos...We insist on one thing: the man of 'primitive' and traditional societies did create the world—the land he occupied, his village, his house—in accordance with an ideal model, particularly that of the Gods that created the universe. Which does not mean, of course, that man considers himself to be an equal of the Gods, simply that he cannot live in chaos, that he always feels the need to locate himself in an organized world, and the model for this is the Cosmos."[2]

And it is this fundamental principle I would like to consider here: that Gaudí's residential architecture—his houses with gardens and his parks—constitutes a real cosmos, a principle of order within the surrounding chaos, an order constructed in analogy and in harmony with the cosmos, with the work of God and His first revelation.

Intrados from the series of spherical-capped domes on the roof of the hypostyle hall at Park Güell. They were all prefabricated with two layers of brick vaulting and then tiled with broken ceramic pieces.

This first principle engenders all the others, developed within the same cosmological and symbolic logic. In order to demonstrate its existence, a detailed description would have to be written. In my opinion, this is the most important angle from which we should examine not only the figurative heritage created by Gaudí in his buildings, but also the way in which he manages to bring about a curious architectural cohesion with general images—apparently without any immediately perceivable logical coherency—and the very constructional and spatial articulation of his works.

The outline I have sketched above should allow the reader to understand the unquestionable religious and cosmic nature of all Gaudí's architecture—particularly his houses, gardens, and parks—and not just the buildings that have an explicit religious function. As a result of Gaudí's method of anchoring his work in holiness, all of his spatial construction achieves the quality of a dwelling. This approach clearly differs from the one used by architects in the Modern Movement, and in terms that I will explain further on.

I do not think that Casa Milá and Park Güell are included on the UNESCO world heritage list merely for artistic reasons, as masterpieces that combine figurative, typological, and technological innovations. Their exemplary nature is rooted in the fact that they represent designs for contemporary dwellings with a much wider scope—designs that are not mechanically repeatable, but rather something to be meditated upon deeply to help us to face the problems of compatible development that currently exist in the world.

As Norberg Schultz pointed out, the term *dwelling* and the verb *to inhabit* are today associated with a wide range of factors that represent much more than simply providing protection for an individual and his family—a roof over their heads and a certain number of square feet available. Inhabiting, he argues, is in fact "finding other beings with whom to exchange products, ideas and feelings, that is to say, experiencing life as a multiplicity of possibilities," "accepting a certain number of common values," and "choosing a small personal world." These three levels designate three types of houses: the collective struc-

Show house on the Park Güell estate. Built by Francisco Berenguer, it was Gaudí's home from 1906 to 1925. It is now the Gaudí Museum-House.

ture, in the city, the public building for common use, and the private dwelling—a place where a person and his closest family members find their full expression. Schultz concludes: "We can also say that the idea of inhabiting a place consists of orientation and identification. We have to find out where we are and who we are in order for our existence to acquire some kind of meaning."[3]

This observation leads us to the mankind/world, mankind/cosmos relationship. The questions "Where are we?" and "Who are we?" have been pressing ones since the end of the last century for a (western) culture marked by a crisis of confidence concerning a certain conception of modernity and its standardizing technological expression. Thus, the first heroic or pioneering stage (in which Le Corbusier, Mies van de Rohe, Gropius, and Frank Lloyd Wright played a leading role) was one that expressed total faith in the myth of progress; at that point, architectural and urban planning was seen as a way of organizing a society that would be an alternative to the existing one. However, since that first stage, the link between architecture and society has once again come to be viewed as a subject brimming with uncertainties.

Thus in the present planning processes, a democratic commitment and an ecological sense of responsibility are actively followed, but there is an absence of ideas—at least for the present. Meanwhile, a principle has been intuited and formulated conceptually: It states that man as an "inhabitant" is not actually related to with the spaces that are conceived on the architect's desk, no matter how elevated their formal and functional conception might be. Their indispensable references are above all the places themselves—territorial anthropological realities that are historically stratified, and in which a certain cultural identity of families, community, and people has taken shape.

It was, once again, Norberg Schultz who placed emphasis on this in the late 1970s. He based his argument on Heidegger-flavored ideas concerning place and on the transposition of meaning of a Latin expression, *genius loci*, to the term *place*. In a work that brought him immediate fame,[4] he formulated the idea that the traditional concept of place in contemporary culture was rapidly dissolving and that this process was manifest both in the widespread social perception and experience of being uprooted and in the figurative insufficiency of most contemporary planning, which fell victim to an illuminist-based functionalism. Many scholars

The Park Güell gate on Carrer Olot.

took part in the subsequent debate, arguing for a new approach to planning that would reclaim this very dimension through regionalism. Such an approach, they believed, would also challenge the increasing internationalization of ways of living and architectural languages. Furthermore, it would be capable of recognizing the value of the local qualities (the vernacular, even) of a planning project.

In addition, Schultz managed to redirect the attention of architects toward the elements necessary for transforming preexisting realities. He did so by questioning whether it was possible to invent spaces in which humans could live in the mental void of a tabula rasa, without any reference to history and to the specific environmental features of each context.

Seen from this point of view, Gaudí was again ahead of his time, able to move creatively between invention and innovation, tending to adjust the environmental and architectural contexts of his projects rather than to transform them radically.

As we all know, his most interesting innovations came, not from a desire to start off on a breakneck race toward a brilliant future, but rather from careful observation of nature and deep reflection on the value of the historical-artistic heritage that he had received as a legacy. I am not trying to claim that Gaudí was untouched by the social and political contradictions of his time, or that his creations can simply be considered as models for the design of contemporary dwellings. It is not a question of setting him up against all the master builders of his age in order to expose their limitations. In the context of contemporary architecture, his role was and is that of someone who left signposts pointing toward areas of investigation which until now have not been adequately explored, but which are (if we have understood his progress of experimentation correctly) practicable. In particular, Gaudí made it conceivable and imaginable, within the contemporary cultural context, for a sense of holiness to be extended beyond strictly religious buildings to encompass the house, the garden, and the park. In general terms, he gave back to the house its quality as a dwelling, a structure that directly influences individuals, shapes first human relationships, and serves as their protective shell (as Bachelard would say).[5] Thus the domicile helped its inhabitants to regain their own inner world; it was a doorway to a sense of privacy that must be respected, protected, and valued.

The contemporary philosopher Emmanuel Lévinas reminds us in the most famous of his texts, *Totalità e infinito*: "In the system of objectives in which human life takes place, the house occupies a privileged place. It is not the ultimate objective, but although it can be sought as an objective, although it is possible to enjoy the house itself, it does not manifest, with this possibility of fruition, its originality . . .The privileged role of the house does not mean that it is the aim of human activity, but that it is its very condition, and, in this sense, its beginning."[6]

Within this formulation, the dwelling is not primarily defined by its geometric spatial extension: "The site of the dwelling," Lévinas explains, "exists as an original fact with respect to which (and not the other way round) one has to explain the appearance of the physical-geometric extension." He continues: "The originating function of the house does not consist of orienting the human being by means of the architecture of the building, nor of discovering a place." It consists of facilitating the existence of an interior space for the individual, of making possible the development of an inner world, a "place/no place," the utopia of the ego, says Lévinas, or rather "a space for a utopia in which the ego can commune with itself within the dwelling," an inner world that enables humans to experience the concepts of "work" and "property."

For the architect who designs dwellings, it is of fundamental importance to recognize the truth of what Lévinas says, because it inverts the Modern method of design, which attributes the value of independent facts to the physical-geometric extension, formally organized in space for the purpose of human life. Identifying the profound inherence of the dwelling in the inner world of the individual, that at the origin of the basic characteristics of the physical-geometric extension of the dwelling is not the architect (despite the advantages of modern technologies and the contributions of the human sciences), but the existence of man—his involvement with the world, his self-consciousness that has been developed within a culture. The architect, in other words, is the interpreter of social life, not the demiurge.

Contemporary architectural planning, in the style of the rationalists and the organicists—that is, as a system of functional responses and a list of material and spiritual needs—implicitly contains a contradiction: It is not a spatial form that follows the development of a person's inner world, but a behavioral model that has been imposed upon the individual.

On the contrary, Lévinas continues, the dwelling represents origin, property, a concretion of the inner world, "withdrawal understood in terms of shelter," retreat, protection, "economic existence," but in a mechanical sense, because "the isolation of the house does not magically or 'chemically' provoke withdrawal or human subjectivity. The terms must be inverted: withdrawal, the result of separation, becomes a specific reality in one's existence within a dwelling, as does economic existence."

I wanted to bring some of this French philosopher's thoughts into certain passages because they describe the sequence of perceptions that I, too, felt when I walked through the interiors of the Gaudí houses—Casa Bellesguard, Casa Calvet, Casa Batlló, and Casa Milà. The intensity of the sense of withdrawal that these interiors provoke, with their variety and fluidity of forms, colors, and lights, can only be described as moving. They generate a psychic separation from the rest of the world; it is not the result of a segmentation between interior and exterior space, or between the different spaces in the interior. Rather it is the perception of the expansion of the inner world that effectively highlights the very presence of the human being within the place.

The architecture of Gaudí's houses encourages the humanization (I cannot find any other expression to describe the experience) of the individual, because it awakens his capacity for withdrawal and hospitality, for individuality and community, for isolation and participation, for celebration and reflection. While the form and space of the house is normally defined (in the experiments of contemporary architects) by relatively few morphological and topological features, Gaudí's creations awaken the memory of a primordial dwelling, which we might call a cave, the mother's womb, the cosmos, the sky, or the sea reflecting the sky. Whatever the name one might give to the feeling that his houses produce, we can all recognize that our memory immediately finds within it the traces of a primal happiness, of a paradise that is not entirely lost.

It is a truly great loss that the interiors of Gaudí's houses have not been perfectly conserved. They have been modified or adapted into what are virtually folk museums that hardly even serve to satisfy the curiosity of distracted tourists. It is a great pity that the pieces manufactured by craftsmen have been dismantled, and that the most poorly conserved sections of the structures have been given an interpretative restoration. With the disappearance of the original features, of the material quality of the pieces and the surfaces, of the fluidity between the interior and exterior space, one loses the opportunity to experience profoundly a fundamental component of Gaudí's designs: that which he condensed into (and using a concept common in the Middle Ages and the early Renaissance) an analogous relationship between man (understood as a microcosm) and the world (as the macrocosm).

The third aspect of Gaudí's originality lies in the continuous dialogue between his buildings and the natural space: the constant relationship between artifice and nature, between house and garden, whether the latter comprises actual vegetation or stone. His interest in the Garden City (an interest shared by Count Güell) forms part of this relationship. However, Gaudí's real contribution to park and garden design does not derive so much from urban planning as from architecture—and this is not because of the surprising quality of his architectural interventions, but because he organizes the natural space by enhancing it with metaphors and symbols. In doing so, he does not denaturalize it; on the contrary, he brings out its intrinsic, natural, organic structure.

Gaudí's gardens are reminiscent of "The Rose Garden," evoked in the first of T.S. Eliot's *Four Quartets*: a place that arouses memories of childhood, but which is also a symbol of a past and a future that are alive in the present: "Humankind cannot bear too much reality. / Time past and time future / What might have been and what has been / Point to one end, which is always present."[7]

For Gaudí, the garden is a metaphor, not of earthly paradise, but of the power of human memory, another expansion of his inner world. Mankind, says Eliot, is unable to bear "too much reality"—that excess of reality revealed by a particular time in history and its future perspectives. In a given moment, however, man is capable of grasping the real intensity of life, seen as the crux of a drama in progress. In the same way, Gaudí's gardens and parks are not places for the suspension or resting of memory; on the contrary, they are lands in which memory is awakened, provoking an agitation of feelings and reasons that lead to a restless search for meaning.

Ideas for Architecture

I disagree with the view that Gaudí's most surprising inventions were the fruit of an instinctive talent lacking in rational analysis, a talent that functioned by means of an uncontrolled drive. On the contrary, I believe he must have incubated his intuitive ideas for a long time and perfected (by means of a constant refinement of his senses and his personal tastes) his most convincing discoveries, until they matured into spaces and images, of which we can only see the brilliant results and the apparently inexhaustible fruitfulness of his invention. What leads me to put forward this hypothesis is, above all, an analysis of Gaudí's ideas, as expressed in autobiographical texts and in improvised reflections collected by his disciples.

Isidre Puig-Boada divided these texts into two sections: one comprises his own juvenilia, and the other consists of the reflections made by a mature Gaudí in the presence of his disciples.[8] A comparison of the first and the second sections reveals the precocious, original, and

Detail of the façade of Casa Milá, built using limestone from Vilafranca del Penedés. The structure is comprised of large blocks joined with lime mortar.

unified conception of architectural planning that Gaudí had already gone a long way to developing in the years just after he graduated. These texts also reveal a definite coherence between his professional theory and practice, a synthesis between autonomous and heteronomous factors of architecture. Finally, the texts show Gaudí's constant interest in two subjects—the house and the religious building—not identified in meaning, but included within the same single perspective of holiness.

Though the buildings he constructed represent the most important reference—an almost exhaustive one from the historiographic point of view—the written sources (a selection of which I am now going to examine briefly) allow us to understand Gaudí's genius and analyze his expressive intentions which are not always manifest in the finished work. In Gaudí's case, these intentions are especially important, given that very little graphic documentation of his plans has been conserved, a fact that makes it difficult to reconstruct his investigative progress adequately.

First, I would like to examine a few passages from his youthful writings, especially those that refer to one of the constant principles of Gaudí's planning. This principle is clearly expressed in a manuscript concerning ornamentation written in Reus, on 10 August 1878; it primarily concerns the church.[9] In this text, Gaudí describes the indispensable unity that exists in architecture between construction and ornamentation. He argues that ornamentation both in decoration and in buildings, demands "the fulfillment of an infinity of conditions which, if they are dealt with in a suitable, organized way," represent a fundamental principle—that ornamentation is superfluous if it is motivated only by stylistic imitation. He adds that ornamentation becomes complicated if it is reduced to an accumulation of "little ideas" which turn it into a resource at once "mediocre and expensive," and that it simply becomes an instrument of damage if it is superimposed onto the "aesthetic composition, making the object overly heavy and stripping it of its nobility and simplicity."[10]

The young scholar had learned about the importance of constructional momentum in architecture from the *Dictionnaire raisonné de l'architecture française du XI au XVI siècle* by Viollet-le-Duc, and he recognized that ornamentation was meant to beautify architecture.[11] It should be well characterized, geometrically structured, organized into large masses, rich in colors, and logical, though not in fanatical rationalist terms. Recalling the rational formulations of the *Entretiens* by Viollet-le-Duc,[12] he says: "Not everything should have to submit to necessity. I believe that the problem is rooted in the following: In order to satisfy the artistic aims that our age demands, we must search for less costly resources, so that our designs do not turn out to be rachitic in quality and so that we have the means available to comply easily with the moral-aesthetic objective."[13] Thus Gaudí advocated a cheaper way of working through the adoption of modern industrial production. In addition, in 1881, only a few years after writing the text on ornamentation, he wrote a two-part article for the magazine *La Renaixença*[14] and in it he assessed the state of traditional crafts in Spain and examined the works on view in Barcelona.

Soffit made up of glazed ceramics and broken glass on the ceiling of the hypostyle hall at Park Güell. This decoration, which takes the place of one of the columns that was omitted, was the work of José María Jujol.

Ornamental soffit by Jujol on the ceiling of the hall of Doric columns at Park Güell. Pieces of broken ceramics, colored glass, and fragments of pottery and porcelain were used.

He declared himself satisfied with the quality of the manufactured products that he saw—fabrics, embroidery, furniture, metal objects, ceramics, and typographical products—and judged them to be "well executed," [though] the way in which they tend to be arranged and mounted does not help them to really stand out." In his opinion, there were "good industrially produced qualities and results that await a wider use"; special training would enable the craftsmen to "convey sensitivity through industrial products" and to lead them to "the path of true originality, not the kind that merely destroys ideas with insignificant variations in form."[15]

The ornamental quality of a certain architecture and of a decorative object demand, therefore, a great deal of careful thought. This objective, says Gaudí at the start of his text on ornamentation can only be attained by developing an intuitive capacity cultivated through the observation of nature, by acquiring knowledge of contemporary advanced technology and the materials available, and by maintaining the continuity (though not passively, that is to say, not exclusively stylistically) of tradition.

It is surprising that this architect-in-the-making should have discovered so early—and with such great clarity—the three main elements of his future approach to design. In this context, he considers ornamentation to be the compositional momentum that enables the architect to take planning not only beyond the logic of financial and functional needs, but also beyond the intrinsic rationality of building. Ornamentation is "essential for conferring character; it is no more than the meter and rhythm in poetry."[16]

The connection between the heritage that Gaudí acquired from masters of the past and the originality of his genius has still not been well established. Inevitably one wonders whether his terms for the unity of principle between construction and ornamentation (which involve all the considerations of rationality, taste, cost, character, color, geometry and beauty) were a precocious personal choice or a filter created during years in which this unity existed as a fact that had not yet been submitted to critical scrutiny.

It is clear, from the text on ornamentation, that Gaudí already believed that the church represented the highest synthetic expression of all architecture components. However, he also focused on the house, particularly on the relationship between the house and the family. He wrote, probably between 1878 and 1881:

> *The house is the small nation of the family. . . . The privately owned house has been given the name of* casa pairal *(family home). Who among us will not recall, on hearing this expression, some beautiful example in the countryside or in the city? The pursuit of lucre and changes in customs have caused most of these family houses to disappear from the city, and those that remain are in such a terrible state that they cannot last long. The need for a family house is not only limited to one age and one family in particular but is an enduring need for all families.*

The short text called *Notes on the Family House (Casa Pairal)* is a hymn to the fundamental nucleus of collective life—the family—to which the house gives shelter, and which is analogous (in terms of autonomy of life and customs) to the unity of a nation, of a people.[17] Within the reference to a paterfamilias and to a property, Gaudí finds stability in time and a valid foundation for values.

The text obviously reflects his training as an architect who understood the need for sanitation and well-being, as well as the antiurban sentiment that had arisen in England and spread across Europe. However, it also reflects a deep-rooted connection with the rural world of the peasant and the craftsman, the world from which he had come. Gaudí's attention was not directed immediately to the bourgeois house, but to the "needs of everyone." He does not hide his unease at the excessive, overaccelerated growth of cities, which uproot many people from the land of their birth and force them to live in rented houses in the "land of emigration." And he applauds the decision to abandon congested city centers for the spacious, light-filled, leafy suburbs.

By advocating the "independence of dwellings," their "good orientation," and an "abundance of air and light" in the design, Gaudí suggests the (almost medieval) image of a building that is half city house and half chalet-villa—"a house which is neither large nor small," a house that "by enhancement and enlarging, is converted into a palace. By reducing and economizing on materials and decorations, such a dwelling becomes a modest home for a well-off family." One imagines this ideal house situated in Barcelona's Eixample (new expansion area), which had recently been laid out according to Ildefonso Cerdá's futuristic, uniform grid pattern, as a response to the demands of fast vehicle traffic and to the homogeneous diffusion of local services.

While Cerdá the urban planner had imagined an urban fabric comprising a combination of well-built, egalitarian, utopian-style residences and theoretically unlimited growth, Gaudí proposed (and within a few years this became reality) the organization of neighborhoods with varying degrees of elegance, "according to fortune and position." With this approach, which combines an acceptance of the modern urban form with a predilection for elegant residential buildings, Gaudí presented himself as a young architect who was willing to serve as an interpreter of the needs of the new city bourgeoisie.

His approach, we must not forget, is not so different (apart from the peculiarities of local history and culture) from that of some of the most important architects of the nineteenth and twentieth centuries, especially Frank Lloyd Wright and the Prairie Houses of his early career. The American architect managed to become the interpreter of the needs of upper-middle-class owners of factories based in the Chicago Loop, who wanted to live in the open fields of the suburbs and to protect their families inside a "home," a concept Wright reinterpreted as the center of a house that generated a spatial expansion through which it was absorbed into nature. During this early period, Wright also used the most varied traditional skills to obtain an architectural configuration that was both antiurban and "modern"—an unprecedented, technologically updated synthesis that celebrated traditional family values. The Catalan architect was considering very similar needs, though in a different culture, a different land, and a European/Catalan economy that moved at a slower pace in terms of innovations.

Gaudí describes his ideal house with precision: It is surrounded by "a wall that contains the garden and is high enough to block views from the street. The wall is crowned with an open-work section." The carriages reach the residential unit (comprising a single constructional block and a garden) by means of a long ramp leading down to a basement floor, from which people can reach the open-air terrace by a convenient staircase. From here, there is a view of "the garden and, between the foliage of the poplars and the plane trees, there is the house," which stands completely isolated and immersed in vegetation.

The interior space meets the requirements of hygiene and sanitation; the rooms are "correctly oriented" and laid out in a "picturesque" manner. In addition, they all have large windows opening onto the garden. There are two dining rooms, one for winter and another

Gallery on the floor of the main apartment at Casa Batlló. Large glazed apertures between sandstone columns have been sculpted into the shapes of plants and bones.

for summer. The north section includes the summer dining room, the study, and other less important spaces, while the south section contains the winter dining room, the living rooms, the bedrooms, and—set apart—the kitchen and the auxiliary rooms. Between the bedrooms in the south and the study in the north there is a "porch decorated with terra-cotta pieces, in which local sparrows nest. In the opposite corner there is a greenhouse made of iron and glass, a winter garden that adjoins with the drawing rooms and that can serve as a living room for big family parties."

Gaudí defines the character of the decoration by saying it is passed "from child down to child." He imagines it with a simple, convenient functionality, defined in all its details; he describes the objects and reproductions that comprise the "family souvenirs, the historic occa-

Show house at Park Güell, which Gaudí bought in 1906 and in which he lived until the end of 1925. The house was designed by Francisco Berenguer (though it was given Gaudí's signature), and was built by José Pardo Casanovas.

External view of Casa Vicens, in Calle de las Carolines. It was built between 1883 and 1888, in a style inspired by the architecture of the Far East. The house underwent various renovation projects, particularly the one carried out between 1925 and 1927 by the architect Juan B. Serra de Martínez.

sions, the vernacular legends, the delicate conceits of our poets, the scenes and spectacles of Mother Nature, all of which possess meaning and esteem."

A house designed in this way has two main purposes: "First, since it is a very sanitary structure, it ensures that the children who grow up under this roof will be robust and healthy. Second, as a result of its artistic qualities, it will provide them—as far as possible—with our proverbial fullness of character. In short, it will make children who are born there into true children of the *casa pairal*."

Clearly Gaudí had read the work, of English writer Ruskin, whose book *The Seven Lamps of Architecture* was the *vade mecum* for European and American architects in the second half of the nineteenth century. Ruskin expresses thus his eighteenth aphorism, in a chapter on "The Lamp of Memory":

> *I say that if men really lived like men, their houses would be like temples which we would not dare to violate so easily and in which it would be a privilege to live. There must be some strange dissolution of family affection, a strange ingratitude towards everything that our houses have given us and that our parents have taught us, a strange awareness of our infidelity with respect to our love for our father, or perhaps an awareness that our life is not for making our house sacred in the eyes of our children, which induces each one of us to want to build for ourselves, and to build only for the little revolution of our personal life. I see these miserable concretions of mud and limestone that shoot up like mushrooms in the boggy fields around our capital . . . I look at them not only with the repulsion of the offended view, not only with the pain that is caused by a disfigured landscape, but with the painful presentiment that the roots of our national grandeza must have been infected with gangrene right down to their tips from the moment that they were planted in such an unstable manner in our native soil."*[18]

Ruskin's moral and aesthetic dilemma was one that the young Gaudí had also experienced: It is well-known that the first steps of his life as a professional architect fluctuated between an adhesion to socialist ideals on the one hand and on the other, various privileged connections with the aristocracy and the upper middle classes, his possible clients. The young Catalan, whose genius was discovered very early on by the bourgeoisie, was not indifferent to the social life of his age, to its contradictions, to the progressive movements, and to the most exciting humanitarian ideals of the time.

In his youthful writings we find an architect striving to define, synthetically and systematically, some of the more profound values of his profession. In the reflections collected by his disciples from 1914 on, we find a man who was entirely dedicated to his trade and absorbed in a series of experiments that were without precedent. This man had thrown himself totally into the work of building the Sagrada Familia, a task to which he dedicated himself exclusively from that very year on. This decision would gradually lead him to isolate himself within his passionate world of symbolism and religion.

Young Barcelona architects sought Gaudí out in the hope that he would explain to them the secret of the connection between imagination and construction that was displayed with utter originality and great innovative force in the works on view around the city. From these improvised reflections, which are faithfully transcribed, emerge features of Gaudí's temperament that occasionally deflect attention from the most exquisitely architectural aspects of his discourse, in particular his moral inclination toward colors that are strong, painful, or joyful; his emphasis on nationalistic and confessional themes; and the urgency of many ordinary structures. By examining the passages most directly concerned with architecture, one discovers in turn (though only briefly) a rigorous development of his youthful premises, which are pragmatically linked to the finished works or those still in progress.

The Mediterranean region—its trees and its quality of light—are the elements of the natural world that the Catalan architect quotes insistently and precisely as references for achieving a non-servile imitation in architectural ornamentation, in the search for harmony, proportion, vibration,

Interior of the large living room at Güell Palace as seen from the room that runs along the front of the main façade. The upper floor, which is closed off with latticework, was where the musicians would play during concerts or tableau performances.

Basement stable at Palacio Güell in Calle Nou de la Rambla in Barcelona. The mushroom-shaped pillars and the helicoid ramp for the horses are made of brickwork vaulting. Built between 1886 and 1888, it was inaugurated to coincide with the Universal Exhibition of Barcelona.

and plasticity. He repeatedly confirms the unity of ornamentation and construction by proposing an interdependence (of a medieval type) between all the figurative and plastic arts of architecture.

By this point the originality of his method of design and his expressiveness had reached maturity. He had gone through all the classical styles—"worked" with them, as he says—and had become aware of the lessons that could be extracted continuously from nature and from the past. But at the same time, he was perfectly aware that he had put into motion a certain constructional and figurative system. He did not know exactly where it was going, but he felt responsible for it. He realized that, creatively speaking, he was fluctuating giddily between a continuity of tradition and his profound innovations, and he addressed these fluctuations from the solid base of a tireless rationalization of the actual investigative path he had chosen.

He had established a clear distinction between statics and architecture, but he knew the virtuoso exchanges that could take place between two elements. He knew, for example, that the static structures that he had invented could also be given ornamental functions, but that this did not justify uselessly superimposed ornamentation or color.

Detail of the main attic of Casa Bellesguard, completely built out of exposed brickwork. The bricks used are called picholines of silo, 10 cm in width, while the vaulting is bonded with long, thin bricks.

He understood all the practical problems of building, the need to supervise the workmen, while at the same time encouraging them to do their very best. He was an expert in the assessment of the delicate balance that was required between the factors of costs and formal and technical solutions. He did not scorn the combination of traditional building techniques with new materials, such as iron or reinforced concrete. When he deemed it necessary, he himself could take on the role of craftsman, thanks to the knowledge he acquired from his family and to the attention that he paid to all aspects of his trade. He was driven by an unstoppable urge to span the whole artistic universe with his experiments, while placing great value on the wide-ranging skills of traditional Catalan crafts.

Gaudí created his own system of geometry, one that still amazes anyone who can penetrate its complexity, yet paradoxically he considered it a tool for simplifying the building process. He researched the system himself, using it to produce figures that we today, with the aid of computers, can appreciate for their refinement and the richness of their sequences, not to mention the peculiarity of static sections with a minimum of formal continuity. For his houses, Gaudí created intelligent functional designs, in which rationality coexists with economy. He made a dis-

tinction between the ideal construction techniques for buildings in the city, those in the country, and those in the mountains. At times he hints at a force that would compel him to devote himself entirely to building the Sagrada Familia, where the interweaving of construction problems (all of which he had dealt with in previous building projects) existed on a whole new scale and level of complexity.

I have already mentioned that, for Gaudí, the house (whether it was integrated into an urban or rural landscape, whether it stood in a compact city model or a Garden City) was a microcosm analogous to the natural macrocosm. In his maturity, Gaudí specifically stated that the religious building is an emblematic figure of the whole macrocosm: It is the sacred mount, the celestial Jerusalem, a structure that brings together all the best of the natural world and transfigures it into an image in praise of God.

In creating the microcosm of the house, Gaudí was not interested in the separation between the dwelling and the context, but was on the contrary pursuing a continuous osmosis, then in the religious building, he could bring all of the natural world into it, infusing the place with a cosmic nature centered around the presence of God among human beings. There is no doubt that Gaudí's creative progress was driven by this belief.

The chimney covers on the roof of Casa Milá. They are built out of flat brick and rendered with lime mortar. Gaudí gave up the post of works manager for this house in 1911, and consequently it is impossible for us to tell what the final decoration of these chimneys would have been like.

One of his many reflections made in his mature years describes the path that this Catalan architect took after 1914–16, when he finished his last civil works projects: Casa Milá and Park Güell. "One day when I was having lunch with the bishop of Majorca," he wrote, "someone spoke about how wonderful it was that images persist in the retina, that magnificent photographic machine, and one of our fellow diners said that of course it was wonderful, because it is man's principal sense. I was surprised and, wishing to speak about this (it was one of those things that one thinks about sometimes), I said to him, "It is not the principal sense, as that is the sense of glory, because St. Peter says that glory is the vision of God—it is the sense of space, of plasticity, of light. The sense of hearing is not so perfect because it takes time. Vision is immensity—I can see what is there and what is not there."[19]

Vision is the sense of glory, it is the vision of God, in terms of sense of space, of plasticity and of light. Gaudí reached this conviction very early on. His houses and his gardens, which are open-and-closed spaces within larger interior spaces, convey with immediacy—in the play of structures, forms, and images—the basic elements of the cosmos: the solidity and variety of the land, the changing beauty of the sky and of the sea that acts as a mirror to the sky, and the horizon and the four cardinal points. The divine presence is transcribed onto the visibility of the cosmic order, converted into architectural order: Everywhere, in paradoxical variety, can be found centers, axes, orientation features, and the hierarchical coordination of spaces.

In his way of seeing, his idea of vision as a sense of glory, Gaudí grasped the connection between totality and fragmentariness, of which I have only been able to give a brief outline here. Gaudí's approach to design, in effect, though it is characterized by a strong rational rigor, manages to carry our gaze beyond this level, toward the perception of glory—if the spectator is willing to let the more superficial emotions evaporate and to allow the time necessary for this glory to be revealed.

Notes

1. Of the extensive works published by these authors, see especially: M. Eliade, *Lo sagrado y lo profano*, (originally published in French, 1964); Idem, *Spezzare il tetto alla casa—La creatività e i suoi simboli*, (Milan: Jaca Book, 1988); J. Ries, *Il sacro nella storia religiosa dell'umanità*, (Milan: Jaca Book, 1990). Ries is also editor (at the aforementioned Milanese publishing company) of a series of publications on the subject, of which we would recommend *Trattato di antropologia del sacro*, a collective work in several volumes, still unfinished.

2. M. Eliade, *Spezzare il tetto alla casa* (Milan: Jaca Book, 1988), 65–66.

3. C. Norberg Schultz, *L'abitare. L'insediamento, lo spazio urbano, la casa* (Milan: Electa, 1995), 7.

4. C. Norberg Schultz, *Genius Loci. Paesaggio ambiente archittetura* (Milan: Electa, 1979).

5. G. Bachelard, *La poetica dello spazio* (Bari: Dedalo, 1970).

6. E. Lévinas, *Totalità e infinito—Saggio sull'esteriorità* (Milan, 1977) 155–77.

7. T.S. Eliot, *Opere* (Bompiani, 1968), 263.

8. A. Gaudí, *El pensament de Gaudí*, edited by I. Puig-Boada (Catalonia College of Architects, 1981).

9. Ibid. From the text *Ornamentació*. See excerpts in the anthological section of this volume.

10. Ibid. Passage reproduced in the anthological section of this volume.

11. E. Viollet-le-Duc, *Dictionnaire raisonné de l'architecture française du XI au XVI siècle*, 10 vols. (Paris: Bauce-Morel, 1854–68).

12. E. Viollet-le-Duc, *Entretiens sur l'architecture*, 2 vols., and atlas (Paris 1863–72).

13. A. Gaudí, *El pensament de Gaudí*. The passage is reproduced in the anthological section of this volume.

14. Ibid.

15. Ibid. The passage is reproduced in the anthological section of this volume.

16. Ibid. The passage is reproduced in the anthological section of this volume.

17. Ibid. The text is reproduced in full in the anthological section of this volume.

18. J. Ruskin, *The Seven Lamps of Architecture*.

19. A. Gaudí, *El pensament de Gaudí*. Passage reproduced in the anthological section of this volume.

GAUDÍ'S TOWN AND COUNTRY HOUSES

Joan Bassegoda Nonell

Access room between the street-side façade and the large living room at Palacio Güell, just as it was when the Güell family lived there. Columns of polished Garraf marble and catenary arches of the same material.

THE MOST SIGNIFICANT PORTION OF GAUDÍ'S WORK CONSISTED OF THE Sagrada Familia and the commissions he received from Eusebio Güell. Gaudí designed a number of buildings for Güell, a wealthy manufacturer, and a typical example of the second generation of the Catalan middle-class ennobled by King Alfonso XIII: the Finca Güell at Les Corts, which became the royal palace in 1925; Palacio Güell on Calle Nou de la Rambla, which since 1950 has been the property of the Barcelona Provincial Council (and in which the Museum of Scenic Art was established); the Bodegas at Garraf, which has now been turned into a restaurant; and the Chalet de Catllaràs, now used as a children's hostel for the diocese of Solsona.

Other wealthy and distinguished members of the middle class who became Gaudí's clients included the Vicens, Figueras, Batlló, and Milá families. In 1890 Casa Vicens became the property of the Jover family, and they live in the building to this day. Manuel Vicens was a stock-

Dining room in Casa Batlló with a view of the rear terrace. The table, the seats, and the wooden benches (all of oak) were made by Casa & Bardés. They were acquired by *The Friends of Gaudí* and can be seen at the Gaudí Museum-House in Park Güell.

broker who benefited from Gaudí's genius very early on in the architect's career. Casa Bellesguard, commissioned by the Figueras family, became in time Dr. Guilera's oncology clinic, and the doctor's descendants still live there. The Batlló family lived in the house on the Paseo de Gracia until 1940, and since then it has been used for many different purposes, at present as a space for meetings and banquets. The Milá family occupied the first floor of the other house on Paseo de Gracia until 1945, and later, when it became the property of the Caja de Ahorros de Catalunya (the Catalonia Savings Bank), it was converted into a cultural center and exhibition hall. The Calvet family sold their house in Calle Caspe to the Llensa Boyer family, who still live on the first and second floor; the remaining apartments are rented and there is a restaurant in the first-floor office space. The Capricho de Comillas, which was built for Máximo Díaz de Quijano, remained in the hands of the family of the marquess of Comillas until it was sold in the 1970s; it is currently a restaurant. Astorga Episcopal Palace was completed by another architect, and no bishops of the diocese ever lived there; it is now Los Caminos Museum. In 1931 Casa Botines in León was bought by a savings bank; it has been restored and is now the cultural center for the Caja España. Park Güell, Eusebio Güell's house, which was partly modified by Gaudí, has been a school since 1923, and it has undergone many enlargements and renovations. Finally, Casa Damián Mateu, which stood in Llinars del Vallès, was demolished in 1939.

When Gaudí designed houses, the comfort of the occupants was always uppermost in his mind. His plans never failed to show great common sense and always provided ventilation and natural light to help create an intimate relationship between the interior and exterior of the buildings.

Owing to the changes that have taken place over time, authentic Gaudí-style interiors can only be seen in Casa Vicens and Palacio Güell, although the Gaudí Museum-House in Park Güell (in which Gaudí lived from 1906 to 1925), contains furniture from Casa Calvet, Casa Batlló and Casa Milá; pieces from Casa Batlló and Casa Milá can also be seen at the Museum of Architecture of the Royal Cátedra Gaudí (a foundation devoted to the study of Gaudí and his works), which is located in the entrance buildings at Finca Güell.

Interior of the main floor of La Pedrera when the Milá-Segimon family lived there. On the death of Gaudí in 1926 the décor was completely changed. At present it is the exhibition hall for the Fundació Caixa of Catalonia.

In terms of housing, Gaudí's architectural production was limited: Fourteen residential dwellings exist, in the town or the country. In Barcelona, Gaudí designed and supervised the building of Casa Vicens (1883–88) at 24, Calle Carolinas, in the district of Gracia. He built Palacio Güell (1886–88) in Calle del Conde del Asalto (now Nos. 3 and 5, Nou de la Rambla), Casa Calvet (1898–99) at 48, Calle Caspe, and Casa Bellesguard (1900–09) which stands in the street of the same name in the district of Sant Gervasi de Cassoles. He also did minor renovations on Casa Clapés (1900), in Calle Escorial, and on Casa Santaló (1900), in Nou de la Rambla, as well as renovating the apartment belonging to the marquess of Castelldosrius (1902), in Calle Junta de Comercio. Gaudí's two magnum opuses in Barcelona are Casa Batlló (1904-06) and Casa Milá (1906–11), which are both on Paseo de Gracia, at No. 43 and at No. 92, respectively, on the Catalan capital's great arterial avenue.

Gaudí also built a number of dwellings outside Barcelona, such as Finca Güell (1883–87), at 7, Avenida de Pedralbes, in the district of Les Corts de Sarrià. This district used to be a separate municipality but was incorporated into Barcelona in 1897. He also built the Capricho de Comillas in Cantabria (1883–85), Astorga Episcopal Palace in the province of León (1887–93), Casa Botines in Plaza de San Marcelo in the city of León (1891–1892) and the house known as Bodegas Güell (1895–98) in Garraf, a village located in the municipality of Sitges. In addition, from 1902 to 1914 he built the gatehouse and his own house at Park Güell and renovated Eusebio Güell's house in the same park, which is situated in the district of Salud de Gracia. Finally, Gaudí designed and built the Chalet de Catllaràs (1905) in La Pobla de Lillet, a town in the region of El Bergadà, and Casa Mateu (1906) in Llinars del Vallès, located in the Vallès Oriental region. In 1904 he also made a rough draft of plans for a house with garden for a painter named Graner, to be built in Calle de Santa Eulalia (today Calle de la Inmaculada, in the district of Sarrià), but he only managed to complete the garden entrance, and it has since disappeared. Thus Gaudí built houses from the start of his career until 1912, when he dedicated his efforts exclusively to the Sagrada Familia, in which he built the small house for the chaplain and custodian of the church.

Smoking room in Casa Vicens. This is an exotic, picturesque, eastern-style design by the young Gaudí, with plaster motifs on the ceiling, paper maché appliqués on the walls and a colored ceramic support.

The Caprice of Comillas (Cantabria), following its last restoration. It was originally designed as a bachelor dwelling for Maximo Díaz de Quijano, brother-in-law of the Marquess of Comillas; at present it is used as a restaurant.

Three works from Gaudí's early period blend orientalism with his fertile imagination.

EL CAPRICHO. In the town of Comillas, Gaudí built El Capricho (The Caprice), which was a bachelor pad for Máximo Díaz de Quijano, the marquess's brother-in-law. The house has a lower first floor for the servants, a first floor with spacious living rooms, and a large dining room next to the bedrooms and the bathroom. It is a magnificent house with a cylindrical tower, the only purpose of which was to provide the occupants with a view of the Cantabrian Sea. It was a true caprice, perfect for a bachelor who was also one of the idle rich. The balcony-

The original gallery in the dining room of Casa Vicens before renovation. Simple swinging wooden trellises provided the open space towards the dining room with shade. On the frieze is the legend: "Oh, summer shade! From the hearth, long live the fire of love! Sun, sunshine, come and visit us!"

terraces are fitted with iron rails that also serve as benches, and when the occupants of the house sat on them, they felt as if they were in the middle of a forest, as the building is surrounded by chestnut trees. The dining room opens onto the garden by means of sash windows, which have metal tubes that act as counterweights and make a musical tinkling when moved. The whole house—with the columnar portico below the tower lined with green glazed ceramic pieces—has a youthful spirit to it, for the architect, then thirty-one, sought inspiration in the architecture of the Orient (this is visible in the tower, which is reminiscent of an Ispahan minaret), as well as in English Arts and Crafts techniques, which he had discovered thanks to the magazine called *The Builder*.

CASA VICENS. Casa Vicens was built for a stockbroker who wanted a house with garden in a narrow street in the Gracia district. This dwelling has a lower first floor, used for the kitchen and the servants' area; a first floor with a large dining room, a stairway, a hall, and a smoking room; and bedrooms on the upper floor. In front of the dining room, a covered terrace, enclosed by wooden shutters, is used for sunbathing in the afternoon. The dining room contains a ceramic fireplace and lemonwood furniture designed expressly for the house and which, in turn, creates the setting for a collection of oil paintings by José Torrescasana.

The walls were decorated with an *esgrafiado* ivy-creeper pattern (*esgrafiado* was a method of decorative engraving widely used in Modernist buildings), and there is wrought ironwork on the wooden tie beams and multicolored papier-maché decorations showing strawberries and leaves. Two terra cotta sculptures by José Riba García, located just above the doors, complete the decor for this unusual space. The adjoining smoking room attracts the attention with its Muslim-style false dome and its glazed ceramic support with carnations painted in oils. A glass lamp decorated with Kufic inscriptions completes this oriental setting, though this lamp was added by the second owner, who bought it in Tangiers. On the upper floor, two bedrooms with plastered walls are decorated with canes, passion flowers, rosebushes and reeds—all plants that Gaudí had found in the little River Cassoles that used to run near the house. In the spaces between the beams, there are pieces of multicolored glazed ceramics representing vine leaves. The garden railings are decorated with palm leaves made out of cast iron, while the façade is partly surfaced with glazed ceramic tiles painted with zinnias; Gaudí found both zinnias and palms on the site before construction began. Captions written in Catalan on the frieze in the gallery make reference to the warm winter sunshine, the pleasant shade in the summertime, and the fire in the fireplace that arouses the flames of love—all examples of charming Romanticism, typical of the age. Glazed ceramic tiles appear in abundance, which gives one a clue that Señor Vicens was in fact a ceramist. Manuel Vicens Montaner had a house in the town of Alella (in the Maresme region) for which Gaudí designed a fireplace made out of wood and metal (now in the Gaudí Museum-House in Park Güell), as well as a wooden corner cupboard with brass overlays, which is currently in the Barcelona house of the descendants of the Vicens family.

FINCA GÜELL. Juan Güell Ferrer owned extensive farm land in Les Corts de Sarrià, and it was there that his architect, Juan Martorell Montells, built a house in the Caribbean style (Juan Güell made his fortune in Cuba and the Dominican Republic). It included a French-style park—with pines, eucalyptus trees, cypresses, magnolias and palm—which extended over thirty hectares. In 1883 his son, Eusebio Güell Bacigalupi, began to purchase adjacent estates and commissioned Gaudí to renovate the house. The scheme called for the construction of two fountains—one dedicated to St. Eulalia and the other to Hercules—an open equestrian exercise ring, a bower with iron catenary arches and wires covered with heather branches, and finally the three gates and their bars. The main gate, decorated with a wrought-iron dragon, is flanked on one side by the gatekeeper's house and on the other by a stable for fourteen horses and a coach-house-cum-exercise-ground covered by a hyperboloid dome. The gatekeeper's house includes a first floor raised upon a stone plinth. The walls are made using *tapia* (adobe bricks) covered with mortar and *Nazarita* Arabic-style decoration, while on the interior they are rendered in plaster. The dining-room ceiling is a Catalan-style hyperboloid dome with brickwork vaulting. The rooms do not have wrought iron tie beams but rather segmental vaulting, the extrados of which is the floor surface for the two bedrooms, which in turn have domed brickwork ceilings. The three domes are crowned with ventilation shafts in the form of chimneys covered with glazed ceramic tiles, and the resulting chromatic effect is surprising.

The two stories were connected by a narrow stairway, beneath which was the toilet. The stables and the exercise ground are on the other side; the former consists of a succession of eight catenary arches that support brickwork vaulting on the same profile to form the central roof section, while the second is a rotunda supported by segmental arches and with fourteen trapezoid windows that illuminate and ventilate the enclosure. This space is completed by a small hall with a bathroom and a stairway with triangular steps, which provides access to the hayloft and the terrace. The groom's quarters can be reached from one side of the stable; the other side leads to the rotunda or exercise ground. This space has a square ground plan that continues, by means of scallops, into a dome with a circular ground plan and hyperboloid profile, crowned with a lantern with a small parabolic dome. The floor consists of rowlock brickwork; in the center is the drain, used when cleaning the horses and coaches, consisting of a circular stone with holes around it and with a "G" in bas-relief. (This initial stood for the surname Güell, though now it is the logo of the Cátedra Gaudí, now based in this building, which contains the archives, the Museum of Architecture, and the Cátedra Gaudí library). The walls of the building are real *tapia* (adobe), a popular traditional building material. Gaudí had requested that Güell bring specialized laborers to Barcelona from one of the rich man's estates in Sucs (Lérida province), where such traditional methods of construction were still common.

The buildings at the entrance of Finca Güell are roofed with Catalan-style brickwork vaulting, without beams of any kind—another method used in Catalonia since the beginning of the fifteenth century. Juan Güell's house and much of the garden were ceded to the Spanish royal family by Eusebio Güell's children, and between 1919 and 1924 the building was enlarged and fitted out to become the royal palace, known as the Palacio de Pedralbes. Now it is home to the Municipal Museum of Ceramics, as well as other departments and offices.

The portion belonging to the Cátedra Gaudí consists of the gatekeeper's house, the stables and the exercise ground, as well as the grandiose wrought-iron gate decorated with a dragon that represents Ladon; he is in chains, after having been vanquished by Hercules before he could steal the oranges from the Garden of the Hesperides. This mythological invocation paid homage to the marquess of Comillas, who died in 1883 and who was Eusebio Güell's father-in-law, as well as being patron to the poet-priest Jacinto Verdaguer, who dedicated to him an epic poem entitled "La Atlántida." This poem refers to the eleventh labor of Hercules—the task of stealing oranges from the Garden of the Hesperides. Gaudí designed this remarkable wrought-iron piece by first using lead strips to make a model and to achieve three-dimensional effects. He had learned how to work with wrought iron in his uncle's workshop in Reus and was a master of this craft.

PALACIO GÜELL. After completing work on Finca Güell, Gaudí received a commission to build a palace for Eusebio Güell in Calle Conde del Asalto (now Calle Nou de la Rambla), in the Raval district, on the other side of the Rambla. This location was chosen because Juan Güell Ferrer, Eusebio Güell's father, owned a house at No. 30 on the Rambla (constructed by master builder Pedro Casany in 1865), and access between the two houses could be created in the form of a covered pathway crossing the interior courtyard of the block.

Palacio Güell was very much admired—and criticized—at the time. It was built between 1886 and 1888, and the official opening coincided with the Universal Exhibition of Barcelona in 1888. Gaudí employed varied and original building techniques in the Palacio Güell: The basement, which is built using mushroom-shaped brickwork pillars and brickwork vaulting, housed the stables, and a series of ventilation shafts in the form of chimneys led from this space to the roof terrace, thus minimizing the smell of horses. The street façade was made of stone

Front view of the elevator shaft at Casa Calvet. The machinery was made by the firm Cardellach, while the carved wooden elevator car with wrought-iron sections was the work of the blacksmiths, the Badia brothers, and the cabinetmakers Casas & Bardés. The columns and the balustrade are made of artificial granite.

from Eusebio Güell's quarries on the Garraf coast. The entrance to the hallway includes two gates in the form of catenary arches enclosed by iron railings, and between that hangs a three-dimensional Catalan coat of arms made in wrought iron. The second floor contained a study, with walls and floors of polished stone and iron beams and main beams. On the main floor, the ceilings consist of a series of wooden assemblies in cypress and eucalyptus, and they function both as decorative and supporting structures. The street façade comprises three successive sections; the central one contains the main hall, which extends upward to the top of the building, where a parabolic dome is punctured with a series of star-shaped holes, which let in light through small windows in a conical structure located on the roof terrace.

The main hall also has an altar which, when its doors are open, transforms the space into a chapel; when they are closed, the space becomes a hall for dances and musical concerts (there is even an organ just behind the altar). This main space is decorated with paintings by Alejo Clapés depicting the miracles of St. Isabel, hung in honor of Isabel López Bru, Eusebio Güell's wife. The main hall leads to the music room. The spacious dining room was decorated with splendid wooden supports, made by Gaudí's friend, the architect Camilo Oliveras Gensana.

The upper floors contain the family bedrooms, and above these the servants' quarters, where decorations in metal and wood anticipated techniques that Modernist architects would use in the future. The roof terrace is simply spectacular, with a conical structure that stands above the main hall and the twenty chimneys and ventilator shafts. The shafts leading from the kitchen and servants' quarters are made of brick, while the others are decorated using *trencadís* (broken glazed ceramic tiles), all of different geometric shapes formed from intersecting cones, helicoids, spheres, and pyramids. In 1910, on the occasion of the Gaudí exhibition in Paris, Eusebio Güell commissioned the architect Juan Alsina to redraft the plans of the building, which were printed on large sheets showing the different models of columns and decorative details. The palace provoked surprise on its inauguration in 1888, when concerts, tableau performances, and religious services were held in the main hall of the palace, all attended by members of Barcelona's high society.

BODEGAS GÜELL. When the palace was completed, Eusebio Güell commissioned Gaudí to construct the Bodegas Güell on the Garraf coast, which lies to the south of Barcelona. On this wild, rocky spot above the Mediterranean stood a building that was formerly a winery, and belonged to the Cabildo Cathedral of Barcelona. Between 1895 and 1898 Gaudí, with the help of Francisco Berenguer Mestres (1866–1914), his loyal collaborator since 1883, constructed a building on top of several stories of underground wine cellars. The new building, which had a triangular section, comprised new wine cellars, living spaces, and, on the top floor, a chapel. The exterior is covered with local stone, which means that the building is perfectly integrated into the landscape. At one end of the top floor, in front of the chapel, an open lookout point is supported by slender leaning columns that follow the profile of the sharply angled roof. The arches and interior vaulting are catenary and the whole structure conveys a definite feeling of balance and solidity.

The chapel has a stone altar, candelabras, and a crucifix made of wrought iron, and above, in a stone belfry, a bell named Isabel, after Güell's wife, is inscribed with the year 1897. A very simple building plan, signed by Gaudí and dated 1895, is kept in the municipal archives in Sitges, the municipality where the building, known as the Finca de Garraf, stands. The main entrance has a highly original iron gate in the form of a net, while the gatekeeper's house consists of attractive stone-and-brickwork forms.

CASA CALVET. Gaudí had already built a house on Calle de Caspe in Barcelona (consisting of apartments between party walls) when he was commissioned by the textile manufacturer Pedro Mártir Calvet to design another. This project was of great interest to Gaudí, as it called for innovative solutions for the model of a rental apartment house in Barcelona's Eixample (new development) district. The building's street façade was made entirely of Montjuïch sandstone, with flagstone balconies sculpted with abundant designs in relief and a complex gallery on the second floor, also with designs in relief featuring mushrooms, since the owner was a mycologist. Meanwhile, at the top of the façade was a horn of plenty with fruit spilling out of it.

The building's basement was used as a storeroom for textiles, and on the first floor there was an office, a shop, the entranceway to the floors above, as well as access to the storeroom. Over the central door can be seen the letter C (for Calvet) in relief in stone and a cypress tree, a symbol of hospitality. The wooden doors have wrought-iron knockers with a symbolic design: They consist of a cross that strikes a bedbug (*cimex lectularius*), a symbol of sin. In the first hall, wooden benches are placed against the tiled walls (the glazed ceramic tiles are a bright cobalt blue), with mirrors and Baroque-style brass lamps completing the décor. Beyond lies the stairway, which is contained between the plot's two courtyard areas; as a result, it is well lit and the rooms are adequately ventilated. In the eye of the stairwell is an elevator with an extraordinary car made of carved wood and wrought iron—a work of art in itself. The second-floor stairway landing is supported by Solomonic columns made of artificial granite, and the walls are painted with vines and bunches of grapes, together with captions from the poetical concepts of Faith, Homeland, and Love. Each floor has two doors per landing for the two separate apartments. The ones on the second floor have a large terrace at the back (above the storeroom) which is divided into two parts, the smaller area being for the rented flat and the larger one for the Calvet family's apartment. The latter terrace space contains large artificial-stone jardinières, decidedly Baroque in style, while at the end there is a rocky fountain, very much in the style of Romantic gardens. The rear façade consists of rendered brickwork with balconies that have artificial-stone balustrades. Originally the plasterwork included *esgrafiado* designs with the owner's initials—P. M.C.—and garlands in different colors. Only a few of these *esgrafiados* remain, as they have deteriorated over time. The top of the street façade is crowned with curved decorations, above which sit two stone balls with wrought-iron crosses. Below are three sculpted heads, those of San Pedro the Martyr, San Ginés the Notary, and San Ginés the Actor, in honor of the owner, Pedro Mártir Calvet, and the patron saints of his hometown, San Ginés de Vilassar. The sculptural complexity of the main façade meant that, in addition to the plans and drawings, a plaster model was required, and Francisco Berenguer Mestres, architect Juan Rubió Bellver, and sculptor Lorenzo Matamala Piñol all collaborated on this project.

A particularly striking feature of this house is the wooden furniture, both in the owner's office and in his home. The office has an oak partition with windows for serving customers. This carving on the partition was done entirely with a gouge, and on the external section (the customer side) two-sided oak benches were assembled without screws or nails. The large cupboards are real sculptures in themselves. The office contained wooden chairs, armchairs, and tables, all carved into organic shapes. These original pieces are now in the hands of the present owners and have been reproduced and marketed with great success.

On the second floor, the *salón de respeto* (a room for special occasions—currently in the Gaudí Museum-House in Park Güell), featured gilded wood, a mirror, and sumptuous upholstery on the sofa, armchairs, chairs, and stools. Gaudí designed some plaster-and-wattle screen ceilings for the second floor, but he was unable to install them, owing to a plasterers' strike. Instead, the owner decided on a coffered ceiling with of standard wood molding that was decorated with paintings of flowers and plants, as Señor Calvet was very keen on botany. In 1900 the city council launched a competition for the best building constructed in the city during the year, and the prize in that inaugural year went to Casa Calvet. A bronze plaque (made by the sculptor Andrés Aleu and the architect Buenaventura Bassegoda) on the main façade of the house celebrates the prize, which was never again given to a building designed by Gaudí.

ASTORGA. Don Juan Bautista Grau Vallespinós was designated bishop of Astorga (in the province of León) after serving as vicar-general of the archdiocese of Tarragona for some years. In that capacity, he had in 1880 consecrated the altar in the chapel designed by Gaudí at the Jesús-María de Tarragona girls' school. Shortly after he had had been made bishop of

Carved oak bench and closet from the office of the textile factory on the first floor of Casa Calvet; these pieces demonstrate Gaudí's great knowledge of the skills of carpentry.

Glazed entrance window to the office on the first floor of Casa Calvet; oak wood carved with gouges, brass door pulls, and colored glass lamps.

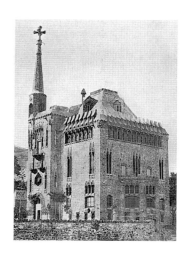

View of the tower of Casa Bellesguard, in the Sant Gervasi section of Barcelona. The building has a square ground plan and an angular tower with a 35-meter-high pyramidal trunk and a dovecote at its base; the features above include a crown, the Catalan flag and a four-armed cross in colored glass.

Astorga, however, the Episcopal Palace burned down, and he commissioned his fellow Catalan Gaudí to design a new palace and bishop's residence. Gaudí duly researched the area's climatic characteristics and the site of Astorga, and in 1887 he submitted his finished plans to the Ministerio de Gracia y Justicia, the ministry responsible for financing the work. It took two years to obtain the building permit, and the first stone of the new palace was not laid until 24 June 1889.

Construction advanced relatively slowly, and in 1893, shortly after Bishop Grau's death, Gaudí resigned as supervisor of the project, owing to disagreements with representatives of Cabildo Cathedral. The building was not completed until 1915, and thus the third floor and the roof surfaces were not the work of Gaudí. On the sections that he did build, Gaudí created a Gothic-style effect by using Bierzo granite on the exterior walls and brickwork vaulting for the interior. The altar structure had glazed ceramic ribs, employing pieces that were made in the neighboring town of Jiménez de Jamuz.

The lower first floor of the palace, surrounded by a moat, was for the storerooms and the stables. The reception area and the offices were located on the first floor, while the bishop's apartment, the throne room, the grand dining room, the attorney's office, and the chapel occupied the upper floor. All of the rooms were very spacious and had large windows. A small garden surrounded the building; it has a spectacular location right next to Astorga cathedral and overlooking the turrets of a Roman wall.

CASA BOTINES. As Gaudí was building Astorga Episcopal Palace, he was commissioned to design a rental apartment house in Plaza de San Marcelo in León. The clients, Señor Fernández and Señor Andrés, co-owned a textile business, which they had inherited from Juan Homs Botinàs. The house was called Casa Botines (1891–92), a mispelling of the name of the Catalan businessman who had established himself in León. Beneath a pyramidal tower roof, the house consisted of a basement storeroom (surrounded by a moat), a first floor for retail, and three more floors above. The second floor comprised two apartments for the owners, while the remaining floors had four apartments each, to be rented. The exterior of the building is limestone with a hint of Gothic: Cylindrical towers at each corner and a slate roof are supported by a wooden framework. The apartments were extremely comfortable and well ventilated, and they received light through both the façade windows and from the plot's two courtyard areas, which had wooden walls. The structure of the house is made up of cast-iron pillars, iron beams, and main beams, and only the exterior walls are load-bearing walls, that is to say, the stories were completely free standing.

CASA BELLESGUARD. In the upper part of the San Gervasio district in Barcelona, the widow of Jaime Figueras owned a piece of land on which there remained the ruins of what had been Bellesguard Royal Palace, a country house built by King Martin I of Aragon in 1410, and which he had named Bella Vista (Beautiful View or, in Catalan, *Bell Esguard*) at the suggestion of his secretary, the poet Bernat Metge. It was in this palace that King Martin I celebrated his second wedding, to Margarita de Prades; the ceremony was officiated by the Antipope Benedicto XIII. This historical content led Gaudí to design a building in a style inspired by the Catalan late Gothic period. The building, consisting of a first floor, a main floor, an apartment and an attic—is made of brick and surfaced with local slate; as a result, the building blends in perfectly with its natural surroundings.

The building has a square ground plan, and the diagonals mark the cardinal points. From the left corner of the main façade, a thirty-five-meter-high tower rises from the slope and, above a pigeon loft, continues up into a conical pinnacle. At the top of this pinnacle is the Catalan flag with its bars in a helicoidal pattern, followed by a crown and a four-armed cross. The crown is colored blue, red, and gold on the flag and white on the cross. This color scheme was achieved by simply applying fragments of glass that were painted on one side and stuck onto the tower using lime mortar. The interior of the building has undulating forms in white plaster on the arches and walls. Particularly worthy of note are the two attics: The lower one has a line of 10-centimeter brickwork-ribbed arches that lead out from a central panel to the façade walls. The second attic is made up of cloister-cornered brickwork vaulting. A circular passage with various flights of stairs runs around this second attic, which features merlons along the entire perimeter of the walls. Gaudí worked on Casa Bellesguard between 1900 and 1909, though the building, the garden benches, and the façade were completed later by Gaudí's architectural assistant, Domingo Sugrañes.

THREE LESSER WORKS. Between 1899 and 1902, Gaudí created three works, though his contribution to the buildings was limited to their design; they were actually constructed by other builders. These buildings were: first, a house for painter Alejo Clapés Puig (he decorated Palacio Güell and the apartment for the Milá family in La Pedrera); second, the plans for a house in Calle Escorial (1899), a structure containing none of Gaudí's features, merely his signature on the plans. When Eusebio Güell's eldest daughter married the marquess of Castelldosrius, she went to live in a house on Calle Mendizábal (now Calle Junta de Comerç), which was built in 1852; Gaudí did the decorations for the second floor; a bay window (1902) in the rear façade with Puntí sliding doors has been conserved. Third, for his friend Dr. Pedro Santaló Castellví, Gaudí designed a house with apartments between partitioned walls, on Calle Conde del Asalto (now Calle Nou de la Rambla), very near the Palacio Güell. This building (1900) does not show any of Gaudí's characteristic design features, either.

TWO RURAL WORKS. In 1905 and 1906, Gaudí designed two works that are worthy of attention: first, the chalet for the technical engineers at the Catllaràs coal mines in La Pobla de Lillet, which supplied the Asland cement factory (1905). The building contains four small apartments on two floors and an attic, all roofed using continuous barrel vaulting with a catenary profile. One striking feature of this building is the semicircular stairway, an ingenious detail that disappeared during a renovation but which can be seen in photographs and plans.

The second work (1906), a detached house with a circular tower called La Miranda, was built by Gaudí in collaboration with his assistant Francisco Berenguer Mestres. It stood in Llinars del Vallès and was destroyed in 1939, though the design drafts have been redrawn and there are plans to rebuild it.

PARK GÜELL. This Garden City project, began in 1900 in the upper area of Barcelona, failed as an attempt to build sixty detached houses. Owing to the distance between the park and the actual city and to the restrictive conditions Güell imposed on the sale of the sites, only three houses were ever inhabited: Casa Trias (1904) was designed by the architect Julio Batllevell Arús and Gaudí had no hand in its construction. Casa Larrard, which already existed on the site when Güell bought the land, was Eusebio Güell's home from 1906 until his death there on 9 July 1918. Gaudí made a number of renovations to the building, including the addition of stone balconies and a chapel on the first floor, though these were disfigured when the building was converted into a public school in 1923. The third house (1902–04) was that of José Pardo, the contractor responsible for the construction carried out in the park. It was built from plans drawn up by Francisco Berenguer, though they carried Gaudí's signature, and it was to have served as a show house for possible purchasers. However, in 1906, Gaudí bought the house (which consisted of three stories with a lower first floor and a large garden) and moved into it with his father and his niece Rosita; he lived there until January 1925, when he moved into the Sagrada Familia.

CASA BATLLÓ. The project involved the simple renovation of a façade, the arrangement of partition walls, and the enlargement of the stairwell for an 1875 building at 43, Paseo de Gracia in Barcelona. Here Gaudí created one of his most poetic and inspired works. A stone tossed into a pond full of blossoming water lilies would produce the same visual

Portrait of José Batlló Casanovas, the client for whom the work was done on the house at 43, Paseo de Grácia, built between 1904 and 1906. He also commissioned José Llimona, Carlos Mani, and Juan Matamala to create the altarpiece sculptures. His son Felipe Batlló Godó kept the altarpiece in Madrid until his children bequeathed it to the Sagrada Familia.

Entrance hall for the main floor of Casa Batlló, at the end of the monumental stairway that rises from the first-floor hallway. The natural light reaches this space through two curving skylights located at one end of the courtyard.

effect as the main façade of Casa Batlló, with its rippling surface decorated with multicolored circles of glazed ceramic pieces and fragments of broken glass in different colors, the exact positioning of which Gaudí supervised personally from the street. This façade has been compared to Claude Monet's series of oil paintings called "Les Nymphes" showing the painter's garden at Giverny.

The double attic at the top of the façade evokes both animalistic and legendary connotations, and people have made outlandish interpretations of a supposed dragon fighting St. George, though the saint is not in evidence anywhere. There is, however, a little cylindrical tower that conceals a spiral staircase decorated with the names of Jesus, Mary, and Joseph which can be clearly seen in marble-colored glazed ceramic pieces (in Gaudí's particular calligraphy). The names are arranged in a helicoidal manner beneath a four-armed cross in Majorcan ceramic, and which is actually the symbol of the Sagrada Familia (Holy Family) and not of St. George.

The façade on the second floor (where the Batlló family lived) consists of sandstone carved with motifs; there are slender columns decorated with plant motifs, elegant woodwork around the windows, and brightly colored leaded stained-glass windows, which are warped in shape. The joy that pervades this design also finds full expression in the bright multicolored rear façade, decorated with a great many flowers made out of broken ceramic pieces that give the surface a cheerful, innocent appearance. This effect is repeated on the chimneys on the roof terrace and in the chromatic harmony of the stairwell, which is covered with different-colored glazed ceramic tiles that gradually become darker the higher you look up the building.

Casa Batlló is the vision of an architect who worked joyfully on a structure that is free of the symbolic complications of Majorca cathedral, or of the bishopric of Astorga or the Teresiana school. If one had to define Casa Batlló, it would be as a sort of architectural smile, an explosion of compositional pleasure created by someone in full possession of his own personal style, an architect who could distance himself from all imitations and from all schools of design, be they contemporary or historical.

Casa Batlló stands on Paseo de Gracia, in a block of buildings called *La manzana de la discordia* (the block of discord) since it contains the most personal works of the Catalan architects of that time: At No. 35 stands Casa Lleó Morera, by Luis Doménech y Montaner; at No. 37 is Casa Mulleras, by Enrique Sagnier Villavecchia; at No. 39, Casa Delfina Bonet, by Marceliano Coquillat Llofriu; at No. 41, Casa Amatller, by José Puig i Cadafalch; at No. 43 is Gaudí's Casa Batlló; and at No. 45 there used to stand the Casa Luisa Sala Sánchez, by Emilio Sala Cortés, who also designed the next house on the same site, for Emilia Adrià.

Casa Batlló was built between 1875 and 1877, and in 1900 it became the property of José Batlló Casanovas, who initially commissioned Gaudí and building contractor José Bayó Font (1878–1970) to demolish the building in order to build another one with a different floor plan. But in 1904 Batlló changed his mind and decided on a simple renovation. There must once have been a country house on this spot, since in the current basement a grotto can still be seen, a space that was used in the old days as a meat safe and which Gaudí conserved, just as he did in his house in Park Güell. In 1970 the building contractor Bayó explained to me the entire renovation process (which was effected between 1904 and 1906) in a conversation that was recorded and transcribed and is now in the Cátedra Gaudí archives. This is a document of great importance, since Bayó was also the contractor who built for Gaudí La Pedrera and the First Mystery of the Glory of the Monumental Rosary of Montserrat. In 1970 José Bayó was ninety-two years old, but he still possessed a strong voice and an excellent memory, not to mention some objects from the sites of Casa Batlló and Casa Milá, which he handed over to the Museum of Architecture at the Cátedra Gaudí. On the terrace area behind the house in Calle Olot (which has since disappeared) Bayó kept a flowerpot covered with pieces of broken glass left over from the façade of Casa Batlló.

The Administrative Municipal Archives contain the basic plans that were signed by Gaudí on 6 May 1904, while in the Cátedra Gaudí a pencil drawing of the façade can be seen. Although a building permit was requested on 7 November 1904, construction had begun before it was granted; as a result, the city council ordered work to be halted, but work continued uninterrupted until the end of April 1906, when Mr. Batlló requested a license to rent out the apartments.

The façade of Casa Batlló, apart from resembling a pond of water lilies, also looks like an exquisite piece of jewelry mounted with precious stones, which are in fact no more than pieces of broken glass provided free of charge by the Pelegrí factory. Decorating the façade with *esgrafiado* or marble surfacing would have made the building work much more costly.

Among those who helped Gaudí on this building project were his assistant, Francisco Berenguer Mestres, and the architects Domingo Sugrañes Gras, José Canaleta Cuadras, and José María Jujol y Gibert (he made the clay model of the candelabras in the oratory, which contained an altarpiece dedicated to the Holy Family, with sculptures by José Llimona Bruguera, Carlos Mani Roig, and Juan Matamala Flotats). The wood sections and furniture were made by Casas & Bardés, who created the organic forms of the benches, the chairs, and the dining-room table. The ironwork was done by Luis and José Badia Miarnau, and the glazed ceramic tiles came from the factories of Sebastián Ribó and Jaime Pujol Baucis.

The bulbous shape (known as the head of garlic) which crowns the cylindrical tower supporting the four-armed cross was made in the kilns of the Roqueta de St. Catalina factory in Palma de Majorca. On unpacking it, Gaudí's workers noticed that certain ring-shaped pieces that formed the support for the cross were broken; as a result, the manufacturer was under obligation to remake the piece. However, Gaudí found this strange cracked effect very

Crowning section of the façade of Casa Batlló. Undulating forms covered in glazed ceramic fish scales in various colors have been incorrectly interpreted by some as being the back of St. George's dragon. To the left, the cylindrical tower containing the spiral staircase that leads from the fourth floor up to the attic, is crowned by the four-armed cross in Majorcan china.

decorative, and so it was left as it was, once the lower part had been filled with lime mortar to give it strength and the broken fragments on the lower section had been secured using bronze nails and washers.

The glass for the façade surface and the leaded stained glass of the large window on the second floor, as well as for the plaques on the living-room doors, was made in the Pelegrí workshops, located on Barcelona's Granvía. The work that was carried out between 1904 and 1906 consisted of enlarging the interior courtyard, completely altering the lower part of the main façade, renovating the appearance of the main and rear façades, and building a double attic at the top of the main façade. The latter would have catenary arches and brickwork partition walling, and was to be covered—on the roof section—with multicolored broken glazed ceramic tiles, while the street façade would be covered with multicolored tiles resembling fish scales, and crowned with a kind of spine ridge of different pieces, some of which were almost spherical, while others were in the shape of split bamboo sections decorated in different colors. Yellows, greens, and blues run from one side of the ridge to the other.

On the second floor (the residence of the Batlló family) Gaudí reconfigured the space using partition walls (some of them curved) and he also decorated the bedroom section. To implement this building project, something other than drafting plans was required: The project team began by making a plaster model of the main façade, which Gaudí gradually shaped with his own hands, transforming what was initially a simple geometric form into the rippling surface of the finished structure. There were no plans for this project, but Gaudí personally supervised the work, giving his instructions directly to the building contractor and the bricklayers.

To make the rails of the cast-iron balconies, a full-scale plaster model was made at the Sagrada Familia workshops, and this model was subsequently used by the foundry workers. The parapet, repeated seven times (plus another, larger one on the small terrace on the fourth floor), was secured to the wall by only two braces, leaving the entire rail projecting outward without any support from the balcony slab, which is made of sculpted sandstone. The parapet has two apertures, closed by means of handrails that are helicoidally twisted and secured to the cast-iron frame with rivets. On the terrace there are balusters of white Carrara marble, also helicoidal in form.

The Montjuïch stone columns used on the second and third floors and on the two third-floor galleries were initially designed using plaster models, in order to profile the slender, bonelike forms decorated with plant motifs. The result was five mouthlike apertures that earned the building its popular nickname, the House of Yawns.

In order to replace the existing façade with the new stone-and-glass arrangement, Gaudí had to prop up the old one (by means of the ironwork on the second floor) and to demolish its lower section. José Bayó recalls that he spent four days and nights in torment until at last he completed the delicate operation. It must be remembered that the building contractor did not have the right resources available, and the entire project was carried out with the aid of a mere pulley and some hemp ropes. An old photograph shows the simple scaffolding made up of tree trunks and boards secured with rope.

In addition to changing the lower part of the main façade, Gaudí's renovations also involved modifying the rest of it: He conserved the apertures and resculpted the exterior brickwork faces, giving them an undulating form. This was later rendered with lime mortar and covered with broken glass in a variety of colors and glazed ceramic discs, also multicolored. Some of these discs were later used to decorate the garden fountain at the priest's house in the Colonia Güell at Santa Coloma de Cervelló.

When the early morning sunlight hits on the façade, it seems to bring the building to life, and all of Gaudí's poetic imagination seems to break into a kind of harmonious, balanced dance accompanied by gentle, innocent melodies. Leonardo da Vinci believed that nature is full of latent powers that have not yet been liberated. The enchanted architecture of Casa Batlló represents the freeing of one of these natural mysteries, with the help of Gaudí's imagination and creative power.

Living room of Casa Batlló as it was when the family Batlló lived there. The teardrop lamp on the central soffit was later replaced by a different one made of iron and glass. The altarpiece, the altar, and the oak doors have also disappeared. At present it is used as a space for receptions and banquets.

In the initial design there was a cylindrical tower in the middle of the façade at the top; however, in order not to spoil the appearance of the building next door (Casa Amatller, by José Puig i Cadafalch [1901]), Gaudí moved the tower to one side and built the small terrace, thus hiding the party wall from sight. Very considerately, he also created a molding that joined up with the neighboring house in a natural, elegant manner, and he ordered a projecting section of Montjuïch stone to be sculpted so that it would receive the cornice of the taller house. Later, several floors were added to the neighboring house, and the cornice disappeared, which meant that Gaudí's complement lost all its significance.

Crowning the façade are the two superimposed attics, which Gaudí referred to as the Hat and the Sunshade. The lower one has a small balcony whose form is reminiscent of an artichoke, and at one side there are the metal arms for two pulleys, to be used for lifting furniture from the street into the apartments. The upper attic contained the water tank. Around the central courtyard, a corridor beneath parabolic brickwork arches leads to the lumber. The courtyard is covered with a kind of gabled skylight supported by iron plate parabolic arches.

This top story was initially intended for servants' quarters and the laundry room, but in 1983 the lower attic was restored and converted into a small museum. The rest of the floor has been accessible since 1998 (when the path of the elevator, which is located in the courtyard, was extended) and can be visited by tourists as an anteroom before they go to the roof terrace, where they can see the helical multicolored chimneys crowned with little conical hats and covered with broken glass on the trunk and multicolored ceramics on the hats. On top these hats were decorated with glass balls filled with sand that had been dyed different colors, though these were replaced during the 1983 restoration by balls of cement covered with small fragments of glazed ceramics. From the roof terrace visitors can also see the rear section of the attic, surfaced with broken ceramics, and an aperture that serves as a window offering views of the Paseo de Gracia; in the other direction, there is a view of the ceramic cross on top of the bulbous Majorcan ceramic structure. For the floor of the roof terrace, Gaudí used pieces of the stoneware mosaic from the old house, though he left the bricklayers to lay the pieces as they wished, without following the original drawings. Unfortunately, this irregular mosaic has not been conserved.

One crucial feature of the architecture of Casa Batlló is the double well, which contains the stairway and the elevator. The courtyard walls were covered with glazed ceramic pieces, some of them smooth, others in relief, in blue tones. On the upper section, below the skylight, the pieces are a deep sea blue, gradually becoming paler as one's gaze descends toward the lower stories. At the bottom, where there is not much light, they are virtually white. If you look out at the well of the courtyard from the first floor, you will see that the walls are a uniform medium blue. It was a logical way to distribute light: a stronger color higher up and a weaker one lower down.

In addition (and following Gaudí's irrefutable natural logic), the windows onto the courtyard get bigger the lower down they are; thus the same amount of light reaches all the floors. At the bottom of each window, there are narrow wooden shutters which, when opened, allow the fresh air from the courtyard to blow in—a very pleasant, practical feature. Natural lighting and ventilation of buildings was one of Gaudí's obsessions.

The second floor, home of the Batlló family, can be reached via a private stairway separated from the hall, by a glass door and the porter's lodge, which is located next to the main stairway and the elevator. The elevator, as well as all the landings on the neighbors' stairway (with its white marble flooring), is protected by a succession of curved iron frames which contain panes of glass with undulating surfaces that let in natural light.

The main stairway leads to an entrance hall, which in turn leads to a room with a fireplace made of a dark red heat-resistant material and flanked by benches of the same material. Framing the benches and fireplace is an arch that shelters this pleasant little nook. This room opens onto the well-lit bedrooms that face out onto the Paseo de Gracia, but it is this anteroom—lit only by one window onto the courtyard—that truly evokes the sense of a cozy dwelling.

The three living rooms can be reached through oak-and-glass doors that are leaded to great effect and have typically naturalistic warped forms. The doors have been treated only with clear varnish, which really brings out the grain of the wood. The central living room has an extraordinary ceiling with helicoidal patterns in relief, as well as a space (also closed off by oak doors) for an altar and a carved wood altarpiece, made by the sculptor José Llimona Bruguera. This altarpiece has a gilt frame on which the word Amen is repeated together with and the letters JMJ (Jesus, Mary, and Joseph), for the design depicts the Holy Family in St. Joseph's carpentry workshop in Nazareth. Above the altar hangs a bronze crucifix, made by the Tarragona sculptor Carlos Mani Roig. There are also candelabras manufactured by José María Jujol and triptychs painted by Juan Matamala. The sacristy is located in a small room behind the altar. Since 1945 it has contained a tabernacle made of gilded and painted wood, which was the work of Juan Rubió Bellver and which is now in a private collection; the altarpiece, however, can now be seen in the Sagrada Familia.

The large dining room is located at the rear of the apartment, with access onto a spacious terrace. Particularly worthy of note are the oak doorframes; the craftsmen of Casas & Bardés carved them by using gouges. All the frames are different, each one a sculpture in itself. They were dismantled in the 1940s when the apartment was converted into offices. Some of the original frames have been conserved at the Museum of Modern Art, others at the Museum of Architecture in the Cátedra Gaudí, and they have been displayed at several exhibitions abroad. During the restoration that took place in 1991, the frames were reproduced and the dining room regained its original appearance, with the exception of the table, chairs, and benches, which were purchased by the Friends of Gaudí and are now in the Gaudí Museum-House at Park Güell.

Between the dining room and the large terrace, two fanlights provide light for the first floor. On the terrace there was a sunshade structure made of iron plate arches (catenary in form and with wires between them) that support a roof of heather branches—a necessity in this courtyard, as the sun can be fierce. The sunshade structure ends on the partitioned wall with a decoration of broken ceramics and with brackets for flowerpots containing prickly plants. The iron

Hall and living room of the main apartment in La Pedrera when the Milá family lived there. The mural by Alejo Clapés Puig was the reason that Gaudí resigned from the project in 1911. In 1926 this decoration was replaced by a different one in a classical style which was more to the taste of Rosario Segimon de Milá.

arches originally led down to large plant pots that were also covered with glazed ceramic tiles and have been conserved. The flooring was made up of pieces of stonework and hydraulic mosaic, taken from the old building.

On the first floor, the façade contains three apertures: the two doors, to the stairway and the storeroom, and three windows, at the bottom of which there are ventilation openings for the basement. The two doors are fitted with wrought-iron grilles painted with ivory-colored white lead with gilt touches. The balconies were also painted with white lead (lead carbonate) to prevent rusting. Gaudí used it on Casa Calvet and Casa Batlló, and he wanted to use it on La Pedrera, though, in the end, he did not.

Once in the hall, the visitor can reach the upper floor by means of a carved wood stairway, which is exclusively for the owner's apartment or, alternatively, by a staircase that leads up to the rental apartments. The elevator, with an oak cabin, is in the stairwell. On the first floor there is one single door, which was the servants' entrance for the Batlló residence, while on the other floors the uprights of the oak doors are marked, not with a number, but with a gilt letter in the center of a round disc. The letters, which are inscribed in Gaudí's personal style, go from A to I. The G is particularly interesting, as it was the first letter of the architect's surname.

On 29 December 1907, the municipal jury for the Best Building of the Year announced the finalists for the competition: Gaudí's Casa Batlló, along with the buildings by the architects Amargós, Sagnier, Falqués, Viñolas, and Bassegoda, was selected. Ultimately, the prize was awarded to Buenaventura Bassegoda's Colegio Condal in Calle Cameros (now Calle Amadeo Vives). The jury declared that Casa Batlló had been "built with an unusual ingenuity. The eminent architect Antonio Gaudí has displayed his feverish inventiveness in the countless Modernist details that embellish the building." The fact that Gaudí had already won the prize in 1900 (for Casa Calvet) explains why the jury opted for the work of another architect.

Casa Batlló became the property of an insurance company after having been seriously damaged in the civil war (1936–39), during which time it was home to a hundred or so refugees. It was restored in 1940 and then again in 1983; renovations continue today.

Interior of the main apartment in La Pedrera, including the mural by Alejo Clapés, the undulating ceiling by Gaudí, and a Victoria de Samotracia, which was added by the Milá family.

Casa Milá in 1911, just as Gaudí left it on resigning his position as supervisor. On the façade on the third floor can be seen the only iron handrail, which was manufactured under Gaudí's personal supervision at the workshop of Luis and José Badia Miarnau.

Casa Milá unleashed the imagination of the caricaturists of the age. The child says: "Daddy, I want a monkey as big as this one." Drawing by J. G. Junceda in *Cu-Cut*, March 23, 1910.

The house is an inevitable point of reference in the architecture of Barcelona, and it has been the focus of official attention for many years: It was included in the city's catalog of monumental buildings in 1962, it was declared a national monument in 1969, and in 1982 the government of Catalonia declared it a cultural asset. The creatively bright night lighting (officially inaugurated in September 1984) further emphasizes the building's architectural and decorative qualities.

Gaudí always designed his buildings by observing the decorative and structural forms of nature and then applying them to the traditional craft skills he had learned and practiced in his youth. As a precaution he made duplicates of most of the ceramic pieces, which are currently stored in the basement as reserves in the event that of any of the original glazed ceramic tiles break.

This mixture of ingenuity, inventiveness, imagination, and knowledge of the geometry of nature enabled Gaudí to create astonishing works like Casa Batlló. The house has been a source of happiness to all those who have lived in its apartments, who cherish a memory of the building's comfortable, beautiful, and useful spaces. Gaudí's plastic sense, the infinite love and devotion he felt for his profession, and the profound spiritual and religious convictions that shaped his life also informed works such as Casa Batlló, which not only arouses feelings of pleasure and admiration in viewers, but also rewards them with a moving, soul-satisfying experience.

CASA MILÁ. At the end of 1905, while José Bayó Font was finishing Gaudí's work on the Batlló family apartment, he received a visit from Pedro Milá Camps, a true gentleman, complete with a cane and elegant manners. Bayó showed him the apartment, and then on leaving Milá gave him a slap on the back and said, "Now we have to start on my house on the corner of Paseo de Gracia and Calle Provenza. I want it done in stone but with gold joints, something that's never been done before." It is true that Gaudí built Casa Milá (called La Pedrera) out of stone, but the gold joints were never more than the whim of a fanciful client.

On 2 February 1906, Gaudí drafted the design of the house for his new client and began his second great civil works project on the seigneurial avenue of Barcelona. One feature that Casa Milá shared with Casa Batlló is the hexagonal hydraulic floor tiles (manufactured by the

Casa Milá during construction. We can clearly see the effect of the Vilafranca stones, carved into bands to create greater movement in the façade, as well as giving it greater structural strength and a unique sculptural quality.

Escofet company), which were initially designed to be laid in the bedrooms of Casa Batlló. The sculptor Juan Bertran, who assisted Gaudí at Park Güell, Sagrada Familia, and Colonia Güell, made a gray wax mold; according to an eyewitness, José Bayó, while he was on-site at Casa Batlló, Gaudí reworked this mold with his hands to create the definitive pattern for the tiles. When the seven pieces of pale green hexagonal tile (hydraulic mosaic in relief) were arranged together, they created a triple pattern containing a piece of seaweed (genus *sargassum*), a seashell (a *cefalopod* from the *ammonite* class) and an octopus (*equinodermus* from the *ophiroideus* class). This piece is still manufactured in dark gray compressed cement, and the city council has used it for the pavement on Paseo de Gracia.

Pedro Milá Camps, known as "Perico" to his family and friends, married Pilar Segimon Artells, from Reus. She was the widow of a rich man who had made his fortune in South America. Although she did not like Gaudí's ideas, to please her husband she lived without complaint in the apartment at La Pedrera. When Gaudí died, however, she changed the décor to a Louis XVI style, which was more to her taste.

Casa Milá sits at the corner of Paseo de Gracia, and Calle Provenza. It is a rental house with a lower first floor that was used as a storeroom and coach house; a first floor for offices; a main, upper floor devoted entirely to the Milá apartment (with an independent stairway through the courtyard from Calle Provenza); and, above, four stories with two apartments on each floor. The main access to these apartments was provided by an elevator situated next to the entrance on the street corner. There was also a servants' stairway at the end of the courtyard. At the top is the attic, built using catenary brickwork arches and used as the laundry and lumber room, while above is a roof terrace with eight staircase exits and the ventilation shafts and chimneys that have made this house so famous.

The façades that face onto Paseo de Gracia and Calle Provenza are made of stone from Vilafranca, carved into huge blocks and joined to the iron main beams and the beams that form the structure of the building, all supported by pillars of brick, stone, and cast iron. Gaudí conceived the apartments as a series of spaces connected to one another by partition walls, with large glazed expanses to light the apartments from end to end. The light floods in through these large windows and balcony windows, which open onto terraces with twisted iron rails. In order to provide a panoramic view of the street, these terraces are three steps lower than the level of each floor; thus anyone in the bedrooms is afforded an excellent view of the avenue—so much so that the treetops appear to be growing into the apartments. The ceilings of the corridors and bedrooms are finished with plaster in relief patterns, all of them different and sculpted with shapes and inscriptions that produce a pleasant sensation of harmony and gentle movement. Nobody who has lived in one of the apartments at La Pedrera is able to forget this feeling.

The Milá apartment contained some flamboyant pieces of furniture in the hall, including benches, a cupboard, and a chapel, all made from oak which had been carved by the cabinetmakers Casas & Bardés. These pieces are now in the Gaudí Museum-House at Park Güell. The rest of the apartment was decorated with stylish furniture and murals by Alejo Clapés, though all this disappeared during Señora Milá's renovations in 1926.

It is hard to point to a common denominator in the houses that Gaudí designed, since they are all completely different. He never repeated any of his ideas. In each building he created different forms, though all of the structures were brimming with ingenuity and constructional logic and were well adapted to the occupants.

But Gaudí never lived in any of the houses that he designed. As a student, he had lived in wretched pensions in the old part of the city, and on completing his studies in 1878, he rented a modest fourth-floor apartment in a house at No. 11, Calle Call, in the city's old Jewish quarter. Until 1906 he lived in various apartments, first on Calle Diputación and then on Calle Consejo de Ciento in Barcelona's Ensanche district. Between 1906 and 1925 he lived in the show house of the failed Park Güell Garden City estate, a building that had been designed by Francisco Berenguer and built by José Pardo. This house was very modestly furnished, and Gaudí never bothered to give it any special decoration, only making changes to the garden, where he constructed pergolas with iron catenary arches and roofing consisting of heather branches. During the last year of his life, he used to sleep in the workroom in the Sagrada Familia, in a bed set up next to his own work space. He created marvelous houses but he preferred to live in Franciscan poverty.

THE PARKS AND GARDENS OF GAUDÍ

Francesc Navés Viñas

Waterfall at Casa Vicens as seen from the rear looking onto to the widening garden of the house. This work, built by Gaudí in 1883, was demolished in 1946.

I N ORDER TO UNDERSTAND GAUDÍ'S GARDENS AND THEIR RELATIONSHIP TO the architecture of his houses, we have to consider three aspects of his work that are strongly influenced by nature: his designs for parks and gardens and his interventions in the natural landscape, his incorporation of plant motifs when decorating buildings, and finally, his use of natural forms when designing his architectural structures.

With respect to the first of these, we will explore the gardens and courtyards adjoining his detached houses and his buildings containing apartments between partition walls. We will also examine his approach to park design using interventions based much more on landscaping (such as his masterpiece, Park Güell, which was initially a project to build a Garden City estate, and the private garden at Can Artigas), his incorporation of sculptures into the landscape (such as his design for the first Mystery of the Glory of the Monumental Rosary in Montserrat Natural Park, which predated "land art" by many years), and the mimetic adaptation of the plans for the crypt at Colonia Güell to the Mediterranean woodland and mountains.

Portico of the crypt of the unfinished church at Colonia Güell, built by Gaudí in Santa Coloma de Cervelló. Brick vaulting in the form of a hyperbolic paraboloid.

With respect to the second aspect, that of floral decoration and his use of plant forms, Gaudí was always very interested in nature: In his youth he was a keen observer of the botany, zoology, and geomorphology of the Baix Camp area of Tarragona, and he took an optional course in natural science in his freshman year at university.

Floral decoration is typical of all European Modernist movements of the age—Art Nouveau in France, Belgium, and Holland; Arts and Crafts in Glasgow; the Viennese Sezession; Prague Modernism; and the Catalan Modernism of the architects Doménech y Montaner and Puig i Cadafalch—and this may explain why Gaudí was for a long time associated with Modernist architecture and landscaping, when in fact he transcends this movement and creates a form of Mediterranean naturalism. These forms and this type of decoration led to what are known as "stone gardens," including the roof terrace on La Pedrera and the sculptures and relief designs for the Birth of Christ façade on the Sagrada Familia, with its cypress-shaped towers, which were the two outstanding works of his career.

The third area deals with the manner in which Gaudí designed the structures of his buildings according to the forms of regulated geometry—the geometry produced by nature—since it is these isostatic forms that are best adapted to withstand exterior forces. The importance of the structure to the form of a building or of any of its particular features is a characteristic of organic or naturalistic architecture, as demonstrated by the mushroom-shaped pillars of Frank Lloyd Wright and Alvar Aalto. In the case of some of Gaudí's mature works, this concept is employed to the maximum degree. Consider the examples of the tree-shaped pillars in the crypt at Colonia Güell, the forest of pillars inside the Sagrada Familia, and the leaning walls of the viaducts at Park Güell, which follow the angle of the natural slope of the land.

Gaudí was well aware that the tree, with its roots anchored in the ground and its particular branch structure, is perfectly adapted to withstand the forces of gravity and wind; the tree assumes the ideal form with which to minimize the different axial, shearing, bending, and twisting forces that may act upon it.

As Gaudí's architecture matured, it gradually distanced itself from Modernism and became increasingly naturalistic. This technique of making maximum use of the strength of the materials is completely in accord with what we currently call sustainable architecture. For these reasons, Gaudí can be considered an architect, a landscape gardener, a town planner, a sculptor, and a painter, as well as a great expert in all of the skills connected with building.

Although, strictly speaking, Gaudí did not have any disciples, his influence is apparent in the architectural approaches employed by César Martinell for the wine-growers' cooperatives—particularly the cellars at Gandesa and El Pinell de Brai in the Terra Alta region, and the forms of certain buildings by Moncunill, such as Casa Freixa and the present Science Museum in Terrassa.

In order to define and study the particular style of Gaudí's gardens and their influences, we should consider the superimposition of styles of the age, the status of garden design at the time, landscaping and town planning in Catalonia (where the greater part of his work was built), and the particular social circumstances of the period. In the history of garden design, the eclecticism of the nineteenth and twentieth centuries made it increasingly difficult to define the style of a garden; often they could only be distinguished using the criteria of composition, climate, vegetation, and functionality. In compositional terms, a distinction can be made between a geometric-rationalist garden, based on an agricultural layout (such as the ancient medieval and Hispano-Arabic closed gardens and those from the Renaissance and the Baroque periods) and a landscaped-naturalistic garden based on the natural countryside, as in the traditional Chinese, Japanese, and English gardens.

In Gaudí's gardens, naturalism and Mediterranean character come to the fore; the naturalism of these gardens is brought out as their very architecture is blended into the landscape. The Mediterranean character is a feature of all the gardens of Gaudí's age, and is expressed in his use of local vegetation, his integration of the garden into the natural environment, and his strategies to overcome the lack of water in summer. Thus the plants used are native of the Mediterranean sclerophyllous woodland: holm oaks and pines combined with hardy shrubs and creeping ivy, as well as certain allochthononus species from other Mediterranean climates such as the mimosa and the eucalyptus, and from subtropical areas, like palm trees. In addition, the large terraced sections used in Park Güell reflect the Mediterranean practice of growing plants on a gradient. Historically speaking, Catalonia does not possess a palace court garden, and the limited number of old private gardens are in the hands of the few existing noblemen and the bourgeoisie, though the latter group tends to prefer architecture as a status symbol.

Horta Maze (1792–1804), in Barcelona—which was a collaboration between the owner, the marquess of Alfarrás; the architect, J.A. Desvalls; and the engineer, Bagutti—is the best example of a palace garden with noble connections. The features of this Italian-Mediterranean Romantic garden are worthy of note: the heavily pruned box trees next to the palace, the cypress maze (the most outstanding feature), two lateral staircases with their bandstand-lookout points, at the highest point a central building offering a wonderful view of the garden, and next to it the large pond, or *safareig*, a typical feature of Catalan farmhouses, used for watering the garden. All of this geometric space is surrounded by a Romantic-style landscaped garden with a grotto-waterfall and water channels, all blending into the Mediterranean mountain woodland. Many of these gardens originally belonged to large farmhouses or old summer palaces and towers in the municipalities around Barcelona, and they have since undergone drastic transformations as they were converted into public spaces. In the days that performances of the Greek classics were being put on in the theater-square at Park Güell, Greek tragedies were also being performed at the Maze.

At the close of the nineteenth century, local government authorities took on the task of creating public parks. At the same time, large-scale urban planning remodeling projects were implemented, such as that of Barcelona's Eixample district, commenced in 1864 by the engineer Ildefonso Cerdá. The Eixample, with its grid-patterned urban planning model, stands in contrast with the Garden City, a more diffuse arrangement prevalent in England and the U.S., and which would be used in the design of Park Güell. The Eixample, by contrast, was designed according to advanced hygienist ideas of utopian town planning, under the slogan "urbanize the coun-

Eusebio Güell's chalet-villa in Clot del Moro, next to the Asland cement factory in Castellar de N'Hug, which was built by the architect Eduardo Ferrés Puig, a specialist in reinforced concrete constructions.

tryside and countrify the city." It promoted the idea of the compact Mediterranean city with buildings aligned with the street and inner green areas, though this idea became extremely diluted when the courtyards of the housing blocks were closed off.

Barcelona's first public park was Ciudadela Park, created in 1874 by the master builder Josep Fontseré. Later, in 1905, the town planner Leon Jaussely drafted a plan to link Barcelona to its newly incorporated municipalities. The idea of this plan was to create green areas, to open up the Diagonal, and to design green routes through the city, though these points were only partially addressed in the later adaptation project. In 1920 French landscape gardener Jean-Claude-Nicolas Forestier, together with architect, landscape gardener, and parks director of Barcelona, Nicolau Rubió Tudurí, began the organization of the Montjuïch Mountain and of some parts of Collserola, employing a *noucentista* Mediterranean style (*Noucentisme* was a Catalan cultural-political movement that flourished at the beginning of the nineteenth century). The Universal Exhibition of 1929, which was held on Montjuïch, represented the affirmation of this *noucentista* architecture, which was parallel to Art Deco in Europe.

Forestier had already created a Green Plan for Havana and another for Buenos Aires, and his ideas had also influenced his disciple, Rubió i Tudurí, who in 1926 proposed the creation of green spaces in Barcelona arranged in concentric semicircles as far as Collserola and bordered by the Besos and Llobregat rivers. To this end, as parks manager for Barcelona he purchased a number of stretches of land which partly enabled him to implement this project, and the results represent some of the best "green space" projects to have been carried out in Barcelona: Turó Park, the Royal Palace Gardens in Pedralbes (the old Güell estate, for which Gaudí had built the accesses), Plaza Maciá, and the organization of Avenida Diagonal between both green spaces. He was also responsible for Guinardó Park (with planning by Forestier) and the garden in the Plaza Sagrada Familia, which faces the Passion façade. In the late 1960s, during the last years of his life, he planned the great sheet of water that lies in Plaza Gaudí, reflecting the Birth of Christ façade, the only façade that Gaudí actually succeeded in building. Forestier also imported from South America many species of subtropical trees which are today commonly seen in our gardens, such as the tipuanas and jacarandas that decorate Plaza Sagrada Familia.

There were two very different concepts of Mediterranean garden design: on one hand, there was Fontseré's Romantic conception and Gaudí's naturalistic approach, based on the landscaped gardens of Alfant, while on the other there was the geometric concept of the *noucentista* garden of Forestier and Rubió, applied to what the latter called the "orange tree climate." These two concepts would have a great influence (and one that has lasted up until the present day) on garden design and landscaping in Catalonia, the Mediterranean coast, and around the world.

In 1940, Lluis Riudor Carol, the architect and pioneer of landscaping in Catalonia, took over the administration of Barcelona's parks; he subsequently built a landscaped garden on a gradient in the area adjoining the main gate at Park Güell. He and his successor in park management, architect Joaquim Casamor Espona, created the best specialized gardens in Barcelona: the Costa i Llobera cactus garden, the Mosen Cinto Verdaguer garden of bulbous plants, the Roserar Cervantes garden, and the garden design of a number of *turons* (small hillock gardens) that had been planned by Rubió. This stage, which lasted until Spain's period of transition to democracy, was an age of great development in urban planning, owing to the phenomena of rural depopulation as people moved to the city, as well as that of land speculation, which led to the disappearance of a great number of undeveloped perimetral areas and private gardens. In 1976 the Land Law was drawn up in an attempt to halt the chaos that had been taking place in the area of town planning; later the Barcelona General Metropolitan Plan was drafted for the same purpose. Then came the public architectural parks of the 1980s (coinciding with the advent of democracy) in which the vegetation lost a great deal of its importance in favor of multi-functionality and symbolism, which was very often rather gratuitous. However, concern for the environment and the rise of the ecology movement meant that after 1990 there was a return to highly ecologically based green spaces which echoed the Mediterranean garden design tradition of the beginning of the twentieth century. This process, which began in 1992 with the Barcelona Olympics, represents the culmination of Mediterranean rationalism: the idea of opening the city out onto the sea and of creating facilities and public parks in the poorest neighborhoods.

During his childhood in Mas de la Calderera, in Riudoms, Antonio Gaudí suffered from rheumatic fever, which prevented him from playing games with the other children. However, as a result he became a great observer of the nature of the Baix Camp region, with its rocks and mountains, its indigenous vegetation, and its fields of almond, olive, and hazel trees, full of insects and other living creatures. Thus nature became his greatest teacher, one that would influence all of his later work. Observation and imagination are two fundamental qualities that any architect or landscape gardener should possess—Gaudí's illness gave him the opportunity to develop these qualities at a young age.

As an architecture student he had worked in the gardens of Josep Fontseré Mestre (1829–1927), who was born in Reus and had managed Barcelona's International Exhibition in 1888. Fontseré designed two parks in a Mediterranean Romantic-naturalistic style: Ciudadela Park in Barcelona, and Samà Park in Tarragona. The first, a city park that was begun in 1874 to develop Cerdá's Eixample district and which has since undergone a great many modifications, features circular walks, buildings which are now used for the Catalan parliament and museums, a landscaped garden with a monumental waterfall and a lake, and the Plaza de Armas garden. In 1872 an international competition was announced for architects to submit plans for this park. Fontseré won second prize with the pro-ecology slogan: "Gardens are to the city what lungs are to the human body." The project involved adapting the park into the fabric of the Eixample, and the city council commissioned him to implement it. Work commenced in 1874. The park was influenced by the Longchamps gardens in Marseille (especially the waterfall), the Lafontaine gardens in Nîmes, and the Luxembourg gardens in Paris. Sculptors such as Novas, Vallmitjana, and Flotats collaborated on the main sculpture, which was a feature of great importance. Landscape gardener Ramón Oliva assumed responsibility for park's vegetation comprising clusters of trees, shrubs, and creeping layers typical of the Mediterranean climate distributed organically through the areas between the lake and the waterfall. Gaudí, who also came from Reus, worked in Fontseré's office as a draughtsman on this project, earning money to finance his studies. He did the calculations for the structure of the cistern building, with its huge water tank on the roof. The water had to be piped to the waterfall and flow from there to the lake, and it was also to be used for watering the park. In addition, Gaudí designed the monumental rail for the Aribau arbor, the access gate to the park and the railings around it, all made from wrought and cast iron. The grotto beneath the waterfall was also attributed to him, and the strongly naturalistic appearance of this piece became a constant feature in all of his later projects.

Samá Park in Montbrió del Camp (Tarragona) was designed by Fontseré in 1881 as a private garden for a gentleman who had made his fortune in South America—the marquess of Marianao and Samá. The park is highly romantic in style and succeeds in turning a dry stretch of landscape into a paradise with waterfalls, fountains, lakes, and grottoes built in imitation of the mountains. A false grotto in the shape of a hill with a waterfall is reminiscent of the section of Ciudadela Park that was designed by Gaudí. It is influenced by the European Romantic gardens of the age (for example, the Alfant gardens in Paris) and would have a later influence on Gaudí's gardens.

Grotto or cave by the waterfall at Samá Park which was given the deliberate romantic appearance of a temple to the Nymphs; this garden, creates a very pleasant contrast with the dry, rocky landscape that surrounds it.

Access Gardens for Houses and Stone Gardens

In the case of the detached house with garden designed by Gaudí for the ceramicist Vicens on the edge of the old municipality of Gracia, the garden underwent several transformations before it attained its present appearance, as a result of the pressure of town planning in Barcelona. Between 1883 and 1888, Gaudí located the house at the rear of the site, so that the garden would be as large as possible. The owner stipulated only one condition: that his own building materials should be used for constructing the house. The garden contained three spaces: a small garden that separated the house from the street, a front garden facing the main areas of the house, and a lateral garden with fruit trees which served the function of a market garden. Gaudí designed a Romantic garden, with circular parterres containing Canary palms and European Fan palms, a fountain made of green glazed ceramic pieces, and a waterfall built from revealed stonework. The wall that enclosed the garden was made of masonry and railings, while the access to the house consisted of an iron gate, ornamented with palm leaf emblems. The façades feature white-and-green-checkered ceramics and brickwork. Some of the ceramic pieces are decorated with zinnias. Gaudí mentions that both palms and zinnias were indigenous to the site.

Two noteworthy elements on the interior of the house are the gallery and the smoking room, both of which have views of the garden. There are striking floral decorations between the wooden beams in the dining-room ceiling, which include relief designs of leaves and the red fruit of the tree strawberry, a typical Mediterranean shrub, while in the gallery against the light could be seen the leaves of the European Fan palm and the Canary palm. In 1900 the house was purchased by a Señor Jover, whose family still lives there. In 1925, at the request of the new owner (who was a disciple of Gaudí), the surface space of the house was enlarged, in accordance with the style of the house. In addition, the garden was enlarged by purchasing the site behind, which led to the house gaining a fourth façade. In 1927 the street (now called Calle Carolinas) was widened as far as the building, so that the front garden was lost and with it a large Canary palm tree and the glazed fountain, though the latter was subsequently reproduced on a smaller scale at the Cátedra Gaudí building (a foundation devoted to the study of Gaudí and his works). The old iron gate was moved to one side of the garden. In 1946, and again in 1962, owing to the pressure of town planning, a large part of the garden was sold, leaving it as it appears at present. The most striking features in the garden are the Canary palm tree, the European Fan palms, and a magnolia bush. To prevent the gardens of such emblematic houses from disappearing, the Heritage Catalogues should include not only the building but also the garden.

Detail of the sculptures on the Ciudadela Park waterfall, which were created by some of the best sculptors of the time. According to Matamala, Gaudí worked on the grotto beneath the aquarium, where there was a curved bench fixed to the walls, and which was a possible antecedent of the bench at Park Güell.

The waterfall at Casa Vicens was initially situated against the wall of the building that looked onto Callejón de Sant Gervasi. When the neighboring land was purchased, and the strip which had been ceded to provide public access had been returned to the owner, the waterfall stood like a portico between both pieces of land. In the distance we see the chapel of the Fountain of Santa Rita. The waterfall was demolished in 1946 and the chapel in 1963.

The accesses to the Finca Güell in Pedralbes and the Garden of the Hesperides (1884–1887), where previously the Feliu farmhouse had stood, were built by Gaudí on commission from Count Güell. The garden contains pine trees, holm oaks, and fruit trees, in accordance with the garden from Greek mythology. The iconographic apple tree is a particularly outstanding feature. According to Joan Bassegoda, this garden was designed in homage to Güell's father-in-law, the marquess of Comillas. Remains of the old enclosing fence can still be seen on the gate located in the present Farmacia garden and in front of the wall of Les Corts cemetery. In the building's front garden the original trees were left untouched, while a dragon-fountain and a pergola dining room (hyperbolic paraboloid in form) were created as points of reference.

Casa Calvet (1889) is an apartment house in the textile area of Barcelona's Eixample district. The most significant features are the combined gallery-terraces on the rear façade and the decoration in stone with mushroom motifs (the owner having been very interested in mycology). Thus the street-side façade features a large mushroom of the genus *morchella rotunda*, with a round morel (*múrgula* in Catalan) and another with a stylized crown: *Craterellus cornucopoides*, the "Trumpet of the dead"; both of these are edible.

The whole façade of Casa Battló (1906) takes its inspiration from the Mediterranean Ocean. Thus the decoration and the colors of the tiles (greens, blues, and whites) make the house look as if it is underwater, like a building from Verdaguer's "*Atlántida.*" In the courtyard, the color of the tiles varies with the height, going from cobalt blue to white. The balconies also look like marine grottos, though some people say they look like skulls or masks from the Venice Carnival.

Gaudí's crowning achievement in the area of apartment building design, Casa Milá (1910), reveals the enormous importance the architect gave to the matter of light in the courtyards. In this building he continued to experiment with chromatics and symbolism—note the rims that protect the openings. Here Gaudí was beginning to develop the warped surfaces that he would later use in the Crypt, Park Güell, and the Sagrada Familia. The plans diverged from the rigid municipal bylaws—for example, the pillar that stands separate from the rest. The façade is like a huge sculpture in Garraf stone on the first floor, while stone from Vilafranca is used for the floors above. The building takes its inspiration from the idea of a mountain or a huge quarry. Gaudí may have been thinking of the mountains of Montserrat, of Sant Miquel

Tree-like columns in the lateral nave of the (post-Gaudí) Sagrada Familia, in the section which one day will be home to the *Gloria* façade.

del Fai, Els Cingles de Frai Gerau in Prades, or Cala Coves in Menorca, though he had never visited the latter. One particularly striking feature is the abstract garden on the roof terrace, with its chimneys that resemble science fiction creations—in fact, they seem to have come straight out of *Star Wars*. The poet Gimferrer christened the roof terrace the "Garden of the Warriors." The latest restoration gave the building back its original color; the chimneys that had been added when the building was divided into apartments have been removed, and it has been opened up to visitors. It is also used for public performances. From this roof terrace Gaudí's other three great works can be seen: Casa Batlló, Park Güell, and the Sagrada Familia.

Gaudí supervised the Sagrada Familia project from 1883 until his death in 1926, and his work has been continued by architects who have come to be known as the Friends of Gaudí. The architect conceived the interior of the church as a forest of tree-shaped columns, and thus the pillars with capitels resemble knots in wood, from which thinner columns sprout like ramifications, terminating in small sections of hyperbolic vaulting that has the appearance of leaves. In turn, the materials from which these columns are made vary according to the load they have to carry: the columns supporting the heaviest loads are made of basalt, followed by granite porphyry and granite, until finally the columns carrying the least load are of limestone. In addition, the form of the section of the columns varies as they ascend—the same as trees do when they grow. Gaudí may have been inspired by the huge eucalyptus tree that stood near his study. The way in which form varies according to height can clearly be seen in tropical trees such as the baobab *(cieba pentandra)* and the silk-cotton tree *(adansonia digitata)*.

Naturalistic elements are present throughout the Sagrada Familia. Note the interior pillars, a sacred forest in which the divine presence manifests itself. In his thesis on Gaudí's naturalism, architect Gustavo Gabarro writes that the shape of the façade includes the form of the humble house-leek *(sedum sp.)*, which is found in the dry parts of Tarragona, especially the stone facsimile reproductions of the vegetation and fauna on the Birth of Christ façade.

View of Park Güell showing the dominant location of the Hill (Turó) of the Three Crosses, which initially was called the Hill of the Mines, since it was an area of iron ore mining. The Calvary arrangement was situated in that spot because its toponym was *Montaña Pelada* (Bare Mountain), which was equivalent to Calvary or Golgotha.

Two of Gaudí's disciples, the architects Isidro Puig-Boada and Joan Bergós, write in great detail about the plants featured on the three access doors of the Birth of Christ façade. The doors represent the three theological virtues of Faith, Hope, and Charity. The Hope doorway, representing the sea, includes vegetation from Egypt, flora and fauna from the banks of the Nile (since it was there that hope for the Messiah was born), as well as the Flight into Egypt. Thus the section includes the papyrus (*cyperus papyrus*), the lotus flower of India (*nelumbo nucifera*), the water lily (*nimphaea alba*), pickle weed (*pontederia cordata*), Surinam purslane (*thalia dealbata*), the bulrush (*Typha latifolia*), the thistle (*eringiiun sp.*)—all of which are aquatic plants—and the vine (*vitis vinifera*).

The central doorway, Charity, features the flora and fauna of Catalonia, that is to say, of the Mediterranean woodland. At the top there is the Greek cypress (*cupressus sempervirens*), the false acacia (*robinia pseudoacacia*), the Judas tree (*cercis siliquastrum*), the hydrangea (*hidrangea macrophylla*), the wisteria (*wisteria sinensis*), the palm (*phoenix dactylifera*), lilies or Madonna lilies (*lilium candidum*), the Japanese lily (*Iris kaempferi*), the water lily (*zantedeschia aethiopica*), alfalfa (*Medicago sativa*), the olive tree (*olea europaea*), the almond tree (*prunus amygdalus*), the apricot tree (*prunus armeniaca*), the peach tree (*prunus persica*), the cherry tree (*prunus avium*), and the apple tree (*malus sp.*). Some of these species are incorporated into Mediterranean garden design.

Finally, the mountain doorway (Faith) includes plants from Palestine, as well as those possessing Christian symbolism: the violet (*viola odoris*), the aloe (*aloe vera*), the apple tree (*malus communis*), and the passionflower (*passiflora caerulea*). However, there are also American species included in this floral collection from Palestine. The museum contains a mold for a passionflower leaf. In 1999, doing research in the Structures Department, garden design expert Noemí Perez and I made a map of all the plant species, indicating their main characteristics. It is not known which part of the plant—the leaves, the flower, or the fruit—Gaudí chose for the decoration of the façade.

Finally, we must mention the crypt at Colonia Güell (1915) and the way in which it is integrated into the landscape. In this project Gaudí attempted to blend the building into the surrounding pine forest by using the colors present in that particular spot. Thus the black and

dun tones of the burned bricks echo the pine wood and the bark of the trees. Green ceramic surfacing that resembles acicular pine leaves has been placed around the windows, and above them blue-and-white ceramic pieces are suggestive of the Mediterranean skies. These colors might also have religious significance, evoking spiritual transcendence. As with other buildings, the geological feature of the grotto in front of the entrance is repeated.

Between 1896 and 1916, the landscaped path of the Santa Cueva de Montserrat (Holy Cave of Montserrat) was laid out, in the place where the image of the Black Virgin of Montserrat was found. It was decided that the fifteen stations of the rosary should be represented, and the projects were commissioned to a group of outstanding architects, sculptors, and ironworkers. Gaudí's project, El Primer Misterio de la Gloria (The First Mystery of the Glory [1916]), is greatly inspired by landscaping: he excavated an east-facing grotto with the symbolic idea that on Easter Day the sunlight would shine upon the sculpture of the Resurrection and light up the back of the cave. This would of course take place in spring, when the aromatic plants of the area would be at their most fragrant and birdsongs could be heard all around.

Park Güell (1900–14)

Designed and built by Gaudí between 1900 and 1914, what is now a Barcelona public park (fifteen hectares in size) was initially created as a Garden City housing estate (commissioned by Eusebio Güell) in a Mediterranean-naturalistic style and containing a great deal of symbolism. That scheme was, however, unsuccessful.

The park is located on the Muntanya Pelada, mountainous terrain in which there is a disparity of approximately seventy meters between the highest and lowest points, and which lies parallel to the great sierra of Collserola. The south-facing park offers panoramic views of the sea, Montjuïch, much of the city, Turó de la Rovira, and Sant Pere Màrtir. The spot is also sheltered

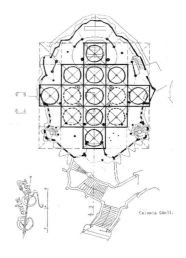

Stairway built into the crypt of the church of the Sacred Heart, in Santa Coloma de Cervelló, before the recent interventions. This church was going to be dedicated to the Sacred Tomb but as it was never completed the crypt was dedicated to the Sacred Heart of Jesus.

Schematic ground plan of the Higher Church at Colonia Güell, the possible arrangement of which has been studied by professors Rainer Graefe of Innsbruck, and Jos Tomlow of Zittau.

View of the land around Park Güell with the Hill of the Three Crosses to the right. In 1906, Gaudí modified the house that he had bought so that he could see the Calvary from the dining room of his home.

from the north winds. The city of Barcelona has been, to a great extent, defined and characterized by natural features: the real city limits are drawn up by the coastline, the sierra of Collserola, and the Llobregat and Besos rivers. The *turons*, such as the Muntanya Pelada, are hillocks that stand just in front of the sierra of Collserola, and serve as the natural lookout points for the city. The areas around these hills became the focus for agricultural development, which in turn became municipalities. These municipalities would later (between 1897 and 1921) be annexed by the city. Today, as the architecture of individual cities is becoming increasingly similar, these natural features, which generally tend to be promoted as green spaces, help define and personalize an urban mass.

The Muntanya Pelada (Peeled Mountain) bears this name because, although initially it was covered with Mediterranean woodland, human activity led to its deforestation. When it was purchased, the only species of trees existing on it were the carob, the olive, and the almond tree (all of which are able to grow under conditions known as dry agriculture). The landscape was similar to that of the Tarragona countryside, with its wild maquis vegetation proliferating over a dry, rocky, sloping area without much soil. Around 1850, a few farmhouses and summer residential houses were built for the bourgeoisie of Gracia at the foot of the mountain, in what is commonly known as the Salut district (though it was then part of the municipality of Gracia). After these were completed, road connections to Barcelona were constructed; at the same time, the Eixample district was created, and city planning was beginning to take off.

In 1899 Eusebio Güell Bicigalupi, purchased an estate from the Marquess of Samá. This mountain land had initially been the property of Antonio Larrard, a banker and industrialist who had built a summer house for himself out of an old farmhouse. Later the estate was bought by the Marquess of Samá. Salvador Samá Torrens, the Marquess of Mirianao and Samá, had

The house of the lawyer Martín Trias, which stands in the only lot that Güell sold in the failed garden-city of Park Güell. A work by the architect Julio Batllevell Arús (1864-1928).

made his fortune in South America, and at that time he was an industrialist and a politician in the liberal party. He was also the owner of Samá Park, the best example of a nineteenth-century Romantic garden in Catalonia (and which has been described above). In 1900 Eusebio Güell commissioned Gaudí to develop the area, with the idea of English cottages and the town-planning principles of a Garden City in mind. Gaudí had already built a house for Güell, the palace on Calle Nou de la Rambla, as well as the accesses and buildings for Güell's summer estate in Pedralbes. The relationship between the two men would last for forty years, until Güell's death; they shared ideas on Catalan nationalism, were both friends of the poet Jacint Verdaguer, and also had a common admiration for the Mediterranean culture of ancient Greece. Güell had studied at Nîmes in France, and some of the symbols in the park might be references to that city and its park, La Fontaine. He had traveled widely throughout England, where he came into contact with the ideas of Ruskin, Howard, and Morris. This would later have a bearing on his idea of building a Garden City at Park Güell. He was a keen participant in Catalan politics and was among those who promoted the Catalonia Regionalist League, founded in 1901 by Prat de la Riba. Güell saw the existence of the Catalan language as justification for a Catalan nation, and he made a great contribution to the Catalan renaissance. In fact, the poem "Canigó" by Jacint Verdaguer, which was highly praised by the Catalans, was partly written in Güell's house. Moreover, Güell and Verdaguer (who was a great walker, or what we would nowadays call a naturalist), traveled together to Switzerland, where they admired the beauty of the mountains. Verdaguer later compared these with the mountains of Catalonia, which he called the second most mountainous country in Europe after Switzerland. He and Güell considered the federalism of the cantons to be an idea that could be extrapolated to Spain. During the Romantic period, nationalism in Europe and in the small states was widely extolled. Much of the symbolism of the park would spring from this Mediterranean-Catalan nationalism.

Great snowfall in Park Güell in 1910. In the background: the house where Gaudí lived from 1906 to 1925. In the foreground: pre-fabricated pieces made for the undulating bench in the Greek theater plaza.

The development project was designed and carried out between 1900 and 1907. The basic ideas for the estate were as follows: to leave 50 percent as a green area and for facilities, and to create sixty triangular plots measuring 1,000 to 2,000 square meters each. The estate was to be enclosed and the points of access controlled. Güell's conditions for development were very restrictive: only one-sixth of the plot could be built on, the rest would be left for a private garden. In addition, a limit was set on the height of the houses, and the planned location of each would be studied to ensure that they did not block the view of the sea or the sunshine. The purchaser was obliged to pay a tax for the maintenance of the public area of the park, the lots were not to be used for industrial purposes, and no equipment that might disturb the peace and quiet of the neighbors could be installed. And finally, no trees above a certain height could be cut down without permission from the planner, to encourage the reforestation of the mountain. Despite these development restrictions, purchasers were given a free hand when it came to the style of the house and gardens that they wanted to build. The work of developing the area was commissioned to the contractor José Pardo Casanovas. Unlike the speculation-based approach to building housing estates that had become common in this country (that is, the sale of the plots is commenced as soon as the streets have been marked out, before even installing the basic services) Güell first laid electricity, water, drains, and telephone services before sale of the plots began. Through the course of Catalonia's history, housing estates (a concept that should have been seen as a wonderful opportunity to create parks and useful public spaces) have always been designed so that the only green spaces are the areas surrounding them. Some commendable exceptions (apart from Park Güell) are the Passeig Maristany in Camprodón, built at the end of the nineteenth century; the Golf housing estate in Puigcerda, built by the architect Bonet Castellana; and the housing estate and road at Ronda de S'Agaró, built by the architects Masó and Folguera between 1923 and 1935.

By 1907 it was clear that the Park Güell housing estate was a failure: Only two plots had been sold, both to the lawyer Martín Trías, on which he built a house for himself, and his heirs still live there to this day. This failure must have been a result of the estate's restrictive regulations, as well as the reluctance of the Barcelona bourgeoisie to move to this area. Traditionally, the city's middle classes preferred to spend their summers in other areas, such as Sarriá, Pedralbes, La Bonanova, and Horta.

In 1907 Count Güell moved into Casa Larrard and constructed a garden around it. Gaudí restored the house and fitted it out, and Güell lived there until his death in 1918. This represented the second stage of the park (to which Güell gave the English name of Park Güell), and many parties and performances were held in the central plaza and the room below the columns. In addition, in 1906, at Count Güell's suggestion, Gaudí moved from Calle Consejo de Ciento in the Eixample district to live in the park. He lived in the show house that Güell had commissioned master builder Berenguer to construct, and which was to have been used to promote the housing estate. Apparently Gaudí wrote a letter to his friend saying that he would like to come and live in Park Güell because the noise and environmental pollution in the Eixample had become unbearable; this is another indication of the way in which his ideas on ecology were developing. Gaudí lived in this house with his father and his niece, who died in 1906 and 1912, respectively. He built a private garden, using features that he repeated in many other private gardens, such as the perimetrical metal pergola (hyperbolic paraboloid in form) with climbing plants such as gardenias and bignonias. The same pergola appears (as an open-air dining space) in the garden at Pedralbes, as well as in the garden of the Sagrada Familia schools, where open-air classes were held. The main part of the house is oriented in such a way as to have views of both the garden and the Turó de las Minas. Gaudí lived here until 1925, when he moved into the workroom at the Sagrada Familia. He died four months later as a result of an accident. On his death, Gaudí left the house to the Sagrada Familia Trust.

Between 1906 and 1909, the Greek temple hall was constructed, and in 1914 the famous glazed ceramic bench in the central plaza was completed; these became the garden's main symbolic features. In 1923 the park and its development area were sold to the city by Güell's heirs, and it subsequently became a public space. Although at the time there was opposition to the city's purchase of the park, it soon became evident that Gaudí's ideas about urban planning and landscaping were so advanced that the conversion of the developed area into a public park was a relatively simple process. From that time until the present, the park has undergone various changes: First, a public watering system was installed, and then Casa Larrard was turned into a public school. During the 1960s, Riudor designed the landscaped garden contiguous to the entrance—known as the Austrian Garden—with the intention of making it into an open-air sculpture museum. At the same time he would free part of a public space that was subjected to intensive use—one of the park's greatest problems. In 1963 the Friends of Gaudí bought his old house and fitted it out as a museum; in 1969 it was declared a National Monument and in 1984 UNESCO included it on the World Heritage list. In 1987 restoration of the park began, supervised by architects Elias Torres and Martinez Lapeña, with the collaboration of Joan Bassegoda and Francesc Mañá. Now under consideration is a proposal to join up the *turons*, thus improving access and adapting the north part of the mountain (not included in Güell's development project), the most important feature of which is the St. Salvador Fountain.

Park Güell is clearly Mediterranean and naturalistic in style; the naturalism is manifested in the way the space is completely integrated into the landscape. The park is not an attempt to imitate nature, like Romantic gardens such as Samá Park. On the contrary, all of Park Güell's elements blend into the environment so that the garden becomes a part of nature. The Mediterranean environment is emphasized through the reforestation of the mountain using Mediterranean woodland species and existing vegetation. In addition, the viaducts make it possible to create typical Mediterranean cultivated terraces—plots of land on sloping areas—while the in-

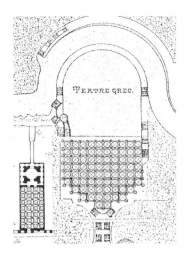

Ground plan of the Greek theater and the hypostyle hall at Park Güell, just as it was published in the report by Salvador Sellés Baró in the 1903 Annual of the Architects Association. When the hall was built, only eighty-six columns were constructed instead of a hundred.

Wall buttresses around the path that encircles the Greek theater at Park Güell. The buttresses support large flowerpots which join together to create a mimetic reminder of the pre-existing palm trees.

troduction of vegetation prevents erosion on the slopes and minimizes maintenance, considerations that are today included in the design of sustainable gardens. Just compare the park with the arid expanses offered by the other *turons* in Barcelona.

Among the public structures of the housing estate that were actually completed, there is the enclosing wall, the buildings, the water cistern, the covered market, and the large plaza. These represent the park's most emblematic areas: the access buildings, the stairway, the hall of columns with its excellent acoustics, the upper plaza decorated with a ceramic bench created by Jujol, and the water cistern that was originally to have been used for watering the entire park. Gaudí built an enclosing wall to protect the whole estate, as it was located at some distance from the city. The surfaced stone wall is crowned with a decoration that is warped and covered with *trencadis* (broken ceramic pieces). Gaudí had planned to build several main gates, but of these he only built the most monumental ones on Calle Olot, though he did draft plans for the one on the Carmelo road. The gate is flanked by two access buildings. The original gate was made of wood, though the current one, which is made of iron with palm leaf decorations, was brought from the old garden at Casa Vicens.

The buildings, with their curved ground plans and warped volumes, are reminiscent of the fantastical Romantic castles of Louis II of Bavaria. On the right as you enter was the gatehouse building with the gatekeeper's house; this is the larger of the two buildings, with two floors and attic space above. On the left was the administration building and the visitors' hall, which was fitted with a telephone, something that was uncommon in those days. The most characteristic feature of both these stone buildings is the warped shape of their roofs, which are covered with two-tone ceramic tiles. The administration building included a tall tower, hyperboloid in form. It was covered with tiles (as were the window frames) and crowned by a huge Greek cross with four arms that point toward the four cardinal points. The mushroom-shaped ventilation towers are particularly striking features. The red ceramic mushroom with white spots on the gatekeeper's building is clearly the toadstool *amanita muscaria*; Gaudí had previously used mushroom iconography on the façade of Casa Calvet. Some of the decorative motifs were references to events of that time, such as the opera *Hansel and Gretel*, which had been performed shortly before at Barcelona's Liceo Opera House—both Güell and Gaudí were keen Wagnerians. The *amanita muscaria* represented the witch's house, while the other structure was the children's house.

A large staircase (surfaced in white ceramics on the risers and the decorations) extends from the main gate in the lower section of the park up toward the large hall of columns. The section beneath the stairway was designed as a parking space for carriages. The staircase splits into two, and in the middle section there are three successive fountains: The first, which consists of a waterfall with grottoes, rocky formations, and water lilies, resembles a Japanese garden in miniature. The second shows the coat of arms of Catalonia inside a large ceramic medallion from which a strange three-armed snake is emerging; from this point visitors have access to Eusebio Güell's house. The third one is the famous multicolored dragon or iguana from the mouth of which flows the water that feeds the whole water system, as well as receives the overflow from the main cistern located in the basement of the hall of columns. The dragon's mouth was the point where the water left the cistern.

The cistern's columns and arches (waterproofed using Portland cement, which was a novelty at that time) are echoed in the eighty-six-column Doric temple. This space was to have been used as a location for a covered market which would have been open two days a week, but by the time it was being built the project for the housing estate was already doomed. Thus the space was redesigned as a location for Güell's parties, since by then he had made his home in the old Casa Larrard, next to the hall of columns. Incidentally, some of these columns have channels inside them for draining the cistern (1,200 cubic meters in size), which could only be accessed by means of a trap door in the ground. In the central part of the Doric temple, four columns were left out in order to create space for a central stage; the columns are decorated with beautiful artistic soffits made of broken ceramic pieces. This central space also meant that large lamps could be hung from the ceiling for use during nocturnal parties. The large central soffits, made out of ceramics and glass in colors determined by the architect and his collaborator Jujol, possess a significant plastic expressivity. The background colors—green and turquoise—evoke the Mediterranean Sea, from which the sun rises, and they echo Aztec symbolism. In addition, the space has excellent acoustics. The Doric-style columns consist of fluted shafts made of rough stone, covered at the base by white ceramics. The capitals are flat and joined to the ceiling by means of domes supported by gently curving beams, also surfaced in white ceramics, which evoke the waves of the Mediterranean with their undulating forms.

Gaudí used a system of prefabrication to manufacture these ceiling features for the hall of columns. Thus the floor of the upper plaza rests on a series of thick cap-shaped pieces that were manufactured on-site, then mounted onto the columns. The whole structure of the hall, seen from the staircase, has the appearance of a Doric temple, with a frieze that is punctuated by groups of four teardrop decorations and lion-headed gargoyles. To provide better support for the weight above, the exterior columns lean toward the load. Not all of the columns stand above the cistern pillars: Some of them rise straight out of the ground. The temple stands upon what used to be the old threshing floor for Casa Larrard. At the end of the threshing floor was a wall that Gaudí used as an enclosure for the temple, and on the same spot there was a magnesia fountain, whose water Güell bottled and sold.

The central plaza with its bench (1914) was called the Greek theater plaza, or the nature theater, as it was the location for open-air performances. It was an unpaved area, so that the water that filtered through it could be collected. The plaza is bordered by the famous bench, which curves to and fro, decorated with broken ceramic tiles. The tiles are green, blue, and yellow on the backrest, while the base and the seat are made of white *trencadis*. The shape of the bench is adapted to the human form, in accordance with Bauhaus principles, and the decora-

The Hill of the Three Crosses, or Calvary, at the highest point in Park Güell. Gaudí had initially designed a chapel with a ground plan inspired by the Church of the Sacred Tomb in Jerusalem, before finally creating a Calvary or Golgotha arrangement in rustic stone.

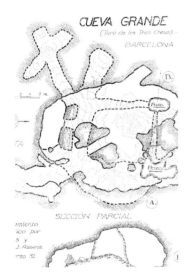

Map of the Big Cave or grotto which lies beneath the Hill of the Three Crosses, and in which iron ore was mined; this used to be smelted in an oven that has been partially conserved in the lower area of the park.

tion anticipates—by many years—the abstract art of Miró, Braque, and Picasso. The ceramic pieces were arranged into words and symbols with religious and Catalan nationalist connotations, though some of these were lost during the restoration carried out in 1989. This bench structure, with its serpentine form, creates both concave and convex surfaces, so that one can sit alone or with others—an example of an advanced functionalist concept commonly seen in present-day landscaping. The bench is provided with drain holes and bumps on the seat to prevent rainwater from collecting on it. At the edge of the plaza, a stone terrace wall runs along the main street, lined with Canary palms.

The park contains thirty kilometers of roads and paths, many of which run along the viaduct-bridges (1900–02), built to solve the problem of the steep gradient. They describe wide ramped curves supported by leaning walls, which were built at an angle to lessen the pressure on the soil. With his advanced conception of town planning, Gaudí separated pedestrian paths from vehicle traffic routes. He created a main road, ten meters wide, which circumscribed the theater plaza, entering from the Carmelo road and leaving the park at Calle San Josep de la Muntanya. A stone wall protects the slope within the area of the theater. In this zone a large number of caves have been discovered, and during construction fossils were found. Gaudí also created two roads, five meters wide, to provide access to the building lots by means of viaduct-bridges. The latter solved the problem of how to overcome the 6 percent gradient without altering the topography. Three-meter-wide pedestrian paths were constructed (with a 12 percent gradient), all of which are joined up by stairways running perpendicular to the gradient.

The viaducts, which are the most emblematic features of the park, serve the twin functions of supporting the roads for traffic above and providing protection (from the sun or the rain) for pedestrians below. They are called Pont Alt, Pont Mig, and Pont Baix (Upper, Middle, and Lower Bridges) and are made from brickwork columns with brick vaulting that is surfaced using prefabricated stones from the actual site. The thick ashlars of the capitals resemble stalactites. The walls and pillars of these viaducts are adapted as much as possible to the angle of the natural incline of the land in order to minimize pressure against the soil and to make the structure blend in with the existing indigenous vegetation. Pont Baix (or Museum Viaduct) is formed out of two rows of leaning pillars in which the column rises up like the trunk of a tree, and a mushroomlike, conical-trunked capital receives the vaulting. These are perfect, natural, treelike forms strongly reminiscent of many of the pillars in the buildings of Frank Lloyd Wright and Alvar Aalto. The Pont del Mig (or Carob Viaduct) is made up of three columns, with sloping exterior ones and vertical central ones, while the ashlars are more regular, with the pillars rising from the base, thus resembling architectural forms more closely. Note the carob tree (now dead), for which space was left in the middle of the viaduct. Pont Alt (or Viaduct of the Stone Jardinières) has ribbed vaulting and stone jardinières containing American agaves, as well as benches that run out to the exterior of the structure.

Near Casa Larrard is the Portico (or Washerwoman Viaduct—a nickname derived from the sculpture on the buttress), the famous porch made up of walls and pillars that lean to adapt themselves to the angle of the natural incline of the land. From the interior it looks like a wave, with a helicoidal ramp at the end. The portico is surrounded by woods containing white pines and a few cork oaks and holm oaks, all of which blend in perfectly with the architecture. In all of the porticoes, what catches the eye is the infinite variety of columns, spires, capitals, rails, benches, and jardinières, all of which harmonize perfectly with the existing vegetation.

The lookout point Las Tres Cruces (Burden of the Cross) is situated in the upper area of the park, on what is known as Turó de les Menes (Mine Hill), a former mining area. It was here that Gaudí had planned to build a chapel for the housing estate, with decoration consisting of three monumental stone crosses that evoke the scene of Calvary. During construction, a number of grottoes were discovered, and within them, fossils. The site provides a wonderful view.

Gaudí wanted hardy Mediterranean woodland-variety vegetation: holm oaks and pine woods and a shrub layer of species such as fescue, mastic trees, mock privets, and ivy creepers. He also combined the forest with the coastal maquis of palms, Kermes oaks, and broom, as well as with aromatic herbs such as rosemary, thyme, lavender, and sage, among others. All of these Mediterranean species are well adapted to the dry summers, adopting the survival strategy of sclerophyllous plants. The woods also contain stands of fruit-bearing trees and plants from other Mediterranean climates. Cypresses rise up from between the crowns of the pine trees, as in the woodlands of Greece. Canary palms appear mostly on the main road, alternating with large stone spheres that delimit the width of the road and the upper terrace wall (an arrangement that some people have interpreted as a visual evocation of Rosary beads), suggesting that after crossing an oasis of desert palms you will come to the Mediterranean mountainside. The carobs and wild olive trees are the results of previous cultivation, as are the agaves and prickly pears, which are American spiky succulent plants used to protect agricultural areas. Among the occasional flashes of color there is the blossom of the fruit trees and of plants whose flowers bloom before their leaves (as if cold winter had been guilty of an oversight), such as the white and pink blossoms of the almond trees, cherry trees, pear trees, apple trees, and the bright pink of Joshua trees. In winter the bright yellow of the mimosa stands out; these trees are typical of the area in Southern Australia that has a Mediterranean climate and can be found in the adjacent landscaped garden. The *Pitospora* are arranged as hedgerow shrubs that define some of the paths, while in the curved section of the Washerwoman portico there is a line of magnolias, a tree common in the U.S., and which produces large white flowers in summer.

For historians such as Bassegoda and Lahuerta, the Doric columns where the marketplace was to have been and which supported the Greek theater were reminiscent of the temple of Delphos and, by extension, the culture of Greece and the Mediterranean. Thus the structure also existed as a kind of tribute to Greece, which had just won its independence from the Turkish empire, and by extension drew parallels with the political situation of Catalonia and the Catalans' desire for independence.

Arched bridge over the River Llobregat in Can Artigas Garden, in La Pobla de Lillet; Gaudí worked on this project from 1905 on.

Can Artigas Garden (1905)

Designed in 1905, this garden was for the private use of the Artigas family; it stood next to their factory and their house. The garden, four hectares in size and adapted to the geography and the wet climate, is located in La Pobla de Lillet, in the region of Berguedá, at the edge of the province of Barcelona off toward the Pyrenees. The garden is very near the lovely town of Castellar de N'Hug, one of the towns in Catalonia that has best managed to conserve Catalan popular architecture. The town also stands in Cadí Natural Park, the sierra of Cadí being one of the few Pyrenean calcareous sierras, resembling the Italian Dolomites. It is also where the source of the River Llobregat can be found, at a spectacular waterfall called Fonts del Llobregat; from which point, the river has cut a deep, narrow mountain pass. It bubbles and foams down through the garden located in this high stretch of the tributary, with that lovely noise produced by fast-flowing water. Near the garden stands an unusual building that used to be the Clot del Moro factory, a structure designed by the architect Guastavino and which is clearly influenced by Modernism and Gaudí's ideas.

Thus the location, which actually serves to define the project, is a narrow mountain pass through which flows the stream that goes on to become part of the River Llobregat. It is situated in the middle of a karstic landscape and surrounded by calcareous grottoes; it also has a riverside woods of pyramidal black poplars (*populus nigra*), and common pines (*pinus sylvestris*) with evergreens, typical of an Atlantic climate. In addition to its landscaping, this garden is of particular interest because it was one of the last of Gaudí's works to be discovered. This must have been because the site was located so far from Barcelona, which has always been the traditional center for all research on Gaudí's work. The garden was first mentioned in a newspaper article in 1971, which makes reference to its style. The same journalist and the Cátedra Gaudí succeeded in finding people from the area who were connected in some way with the work. These included a builder who had worked for the textile manufacturer Artigas and people from the town who remembered seeing Gaudí and who recalled that plants had been brought there from Park Güell. In 1982, during the fourth doctorate course for the Cátedra Gaudí, architect Josep Lluis Dalmau Miralles redrafted the plans for the garden and presented a description of them. In 1989 the town council of La Pobla de Lillet, which had rented out the garden, commissioned the Cátedra Gaudí to research and restore the garden. In 1995 architect Joan Bassegoda restored it, and it has become an important feature in the process of converting the industrial region of Berguedà into a tourist area. The Polish architect-scholar Witold Burkiewciz, when he was redrafting the detailed plans of the garden, met by chance someone who had worked in the home of the Artigas family and who remembered some of Gaudí's sketches, which the architect had drafted when he spent two days in the house. They were drawn on large sheets of paper but had been destroyed during the Spanish Civil War. Thus it seems we can conclude that Gaudí was the creator of this work, in spite of the absence of any written documents.

In 1905 Gaudí stayed in the house of the textile manufacturer Joan Artigas Alart for two days, while he was supervising the construction of a small chalet on the sierra of Catllaràs for the engineers working in the lignite mines belonging to the Asland Company (owned by Eusebio Güell). During his stay, Artigas commissioned him to design a garden next to the factory. Gaudí chose the site next to the rocky watercourse of a tributary of the River Llobregat. He drafted the outline of the project and later sent a builder from Barcelona (one of the team that had been working with José Pardo, the builder of Park Güell). This builder spent six months constructing the grotto by the factory, and the rest of the garden was completed by a local builder (who had been collaborating with the first builder from Barcelona) working from Gaudí's plans. The work was completed in 1910.

In this project Gaudí worked with the same concepts that he used for Park Güell, but adapted them to a wet climate with damp vegetation and made use of the mountain pass-valley structure. One similarity between the two projects is the calcareous rock, which crops out at both Park Güell and in the mountains of the Baix Camp region in Tarragona. One of the garden's most striking features is the grotto, from which flows the water of the magnesia fountain (and which gives the garden its name). This fountain is flanked by two stone benches, and the grotto contains two apertures that provide a view of the river. It is constructed using large unsculpted stones which are given pencil arches, like the viaducts in Park Güell. There is evidence that a similar fountain existed in Park Güell and that Eusebio Güell bottled and sold its water. There are also three bridges that cross the stream: The first, which is also the lowest, is situated by the factory and existed before the garden was created. The second is reached by following the path from the grotto; it connects two areas of very different levels and is formed by an arch which, once it reaches the bank (by means of a few steps), provides access to La Glorieta lookout point. This structure, which is cylindrical with a conical stone roof, offers a view of the whole garden and is the most emblematic feature of the site. A balustrade leads on to the third bridge, which is a horizontal slab with a single arch connecting the garden to a pleasant rest area with benches and tables. The two new bridges are surfaced with stones, while the reinforced cement rails, in the shape of branches, continue along the whole path. These are typical features of Romantic gardens and can also be seen on the bridge over the large pond at Samá Park, which was constructed in parallel with Ciudadela Park, a fact that Gaudí, who had worked as an assistant to Fontseré during the construction of the latter, must have been aware of. Some stretches of path feature rails made of small stones, mounted on metal struts. The jardinières, which are also surfaced with stone, stand above the sturdy stone uprights of the rails, some of which resemble the upper viaduct at Park Güell. On the third bridge these uprights form longitudinal stone arches that resemble pergolas.

Of the stone sculptures, two caryatids stand out: They are located at the entrance of the third bridge and recall the ones near the buttresses of the leaning viaduct (the Washerwoman) at Park Güell. A majestic eagle presides over the final section of the stairway of the second bridge—another example of the mythological and Christian symbolism which is characteristic of Gaudí's work. The Atlantic climate of the park, with its stands of common pines and ever-

The River Llobregat, the source of which is only a few kilometers farther up, flows under the first bridge with a flying buttress arch that stands by the ancient poplars in Can Artigas Garden, which is at La Pobla de Lillet. Recently restored, this garden is now municipal property.

greens, means that the garden varies greatly with the seasons. Autumn is heralded by the yellowing tops of the rows of black poplars, which weave down between the white foaming river and the rocks, together with the red, orange, and yellow tones of the cherry trees, maples, and oaks, and the blue-green of the pines. In winter, the restrained, leafless pyramidal shape of the poplars accentuates the grandiosity of the rocks in the garden. Meanwhile, in spring, the light-green of the poplars and the other evergreens softens the effect of the sienna-ochre color of the rocks and the pine woods.

In addition, the narrowness of the garden and its east-west orientation (perpendicular to the watercourse) means that the dark shadows, which lengthen as the sun moves westward completely change the appearance of the space. And in winter, when the sun's rays take on a more horizontal angle, this contrast is even greater.

As for the vegetation introduced into the garden, Gaudí searched for garden plants that had forms similar to those of Park Güell. Thus, in the jardinières at the third bridge in the garden, he swapped the American agaves he had planted in the stone pots by the upper viaduct at Park Güell for yuccas—another exotic species (also from North America) but one that is more able to withstand the cold. He also used wisteria on the pergola and tall European Fan palms (*Trachicarpus fortunei*) instead of the Canary palms of Park Güell. These tall palms originate from the subalpine mountains of Japan. Of course it would have been advisable to use garden species from an Atlantic climate, but a typical mistake of landscape gardeners is their desire to take concepts and species from one climate and apply them in another. For example, Brazilian landscape gardener Burle Marx began creating gardens in the tropical area of his country using European concepts and vegetation, and it was not until he traveled to Europe that he saw—in Berlin—how beautiful the tropical flora of his own country was, and he subsequently started to use these plants in his gardens in Brasilia, adopting a chromatic, naturalistic approach to garden design that became known internationally as the Tropical Garden.

The architect Ribas Piera, in his book *Gardens of Catalonia*, states that the Can Artigas garden is extremely Romantic in style and that it is a garden worthy of King Louis II of Bavaria. He also mentions that the most important elements are the preexisting natural features, and that the skills Gaudí showed at Park Güell are not in evidence here. In my opinion, this was because the area was not the sort of landscape that Gaudí was accustomed to working in, and in addition, he only stayed in the area for a short time. However, it is without any doubt a garden of great sculptural beauty, and which was created simultaneously with Park Güell. Joan Bassegoda points out certain significant contrasting details and similarities between the two spaces in his book *Gaudí's Gardens*. The contrasts include size (Park Güell is fourteen hectares versus the four hectares at Can Artigas); use (Park Güell was for public use, while Can Artigas was private); and climate (the former was a very dry area with water supplied only by an underground cistern, while in Can Artigas water would become the central design feature). I would add another difference: that of the vegetation of the two environments. Park Güell is characterized by Mediterranean vegetation that does not change much with the seasons, apart from a short period of flowers and blossom; by contrast, Can Artigas garden has a powerful chromatic impact produced by the evergreens. Finally, with respect to stylistic similarities between the two areas, I would point to the use of stone surfacing and the shapes of some of the jardinières and sculptures.

GAUDÍ AND THE CATALAN
CRAFTSMEN OF HIS TIME

Joan Morell Núñez

Rear façade of Palacio Güell. Bond of Garraf stone. Gallery with wooden Venetian blinds on the main floor and balcony covered with wooden sun-shelter. In the upper section we can see the chimneys decorated with ceramic pieces and the perforated cone that allows the light into the large living room.

CATALAN MODERNISM, LIKE ALL OF ITS EUROPEAN EQUIVALENTS (Art Nouveau, Jugendstil, Liberty, Arts and Crafts, Sezession, as well as Baroque art), involved the complete integration of all the different arts—architecture, sculpture, and painting—and gave priority to handcrafted methods over the increasingly depersonalized industrial production of the age. Thus, Catalan Modernism could not have come into existence without the work of the highly qualified craftsmen of that time, who interpreted and manufactured everything that the architects drafted as plans and simple sketches.

The relationship between Gaudí and his craftsmen was a very special one: His building sites functioned just as the workshops in medieval times used to, and he himself was responsible for coordinating the craftsmen. He would check the quality of their work and occasionally supervise it personally, to ensure that it was perfectly suited to its location. Nowadays this is impossible, just as it is impossible to request a slight alteration in the manufacture of any industrial product. Today architects are obliged to adapt completely to what the industry produces, and not vice versa; they have to design buildings using the materials that mass production can offer, and this factor has a negative effect on the creativity of the architect.

However, Gaudí's works are all unique, like any other handcrafted piece of work, since they were designed for different needs and uses, and are so well adapted to their surroundings that they seem to have stood there for centuries. The harmony between the various components is absolute and monolithic, like a sculpture: Nothing is superfluous, nothing is lacking, and the structures are free of any unnecessary ornamentation. Their form can be compared to that of a birds or an airplane, both designed exclusively for flying. All the elements of Gaudí's buildings blend and harmonize like the different musical instruments in an orchestra, or like the components of a Gothic cathedral, where the main façade can be taken in with just one glance: looking up, we can admire the delicate sculptures of its portals, but these play the same role as the rest of the stones.

This is true of all of his buildings—churches and the houses, Finca Güell and Palacio Güell, Casa Vicens, Casa Calvet, Casa Batlló, and Casa Milá. Stone, ceramics, glass, iron, and wood are all integrated to such an extent that when the building is completed, it becomes impossible to separate them.

The relationship between Gaudí and his craftsmen was one of complete trust, as the architect knew that he could expect the best performance from his workers and from the materials he used. Gaudí used to give them a model, which he had made himself, of the work that was to be done. Sometimes this model was life-size, sometimes (especially for his early works) it would be accompanied by a detailed report that included all the information about the manufacture of each piece, including the polychromy. This ensured that there was no danger of improvisation or misinterpretation. In addition, if a piece that he had ordered did not satisfy him, he would send it back to be remade.

It is widely known that Gaudí was himself capable of manufacturing most of the pieces that he designed. He was not just a theorist who left the workers to solve all the problems for him; on the contrary, he knew exactly what he could demand from them and if one of the craftsmen—whether he was a blacksmith, carpenter, locksmith, or builder—was unsure of what exactly was required, the architect could even demonstrate the procedure manually. All the craftsmen witnessed Gaudí's practical skills and saw the surprising simplicity of most of the pieces he commissioned.

Naturally, Gaudí would never have finished any of his marvelous buildings if he had had to make and assemble all of the handcrafted pieces on his own. Thus he entrusted the work to a small group of very highly skilled craftsmen, who worked with him throughout his career, from 1878 to 1926. He always used the same men, whom he trusted and felt comfortable with. With this policy, Gaudí had no need to train workers for each new commission, as he would always commission work from the same firms. Over the years, these businesses lost and gained craftsmen as some retired or died while young ones were taken on as apprentices. Ráfols has already brought to our attention the difference between the work produced by these master craftsmen when they were employed by Gaudí and the work they did when working on their own.

Of all the craftsmen who collaborated with the Catalan architect, José María Jujol y Gibert (1879–1949) was especially important. He was an architect, but he never worked in that capacity with Gaudí: He worked only as a craftsman for him, from 1906 on. Jujol was a magnificent craftsmen who possessed a total command of color. Nowadays great attention is paid—quite rightly—not only to his works as one of Gaudí's collaborators, but also to all the others which he was to create later when working on his own.

Of all of Gaudí's architect-disciples, it was Jujol, without doubt, whose work was most similar to his master's, though he never managed to equal him. This becomes clear by simply comparing their work, though this does not mean that Jujol did not produce work of great quality. Rather, it demonstrates that Jujol's craftsmanship was of a high quality and produced with great artistic sensitivity; he merely failed to reach the level of the greatest of the great architects/builders/decorators of all time—Antonio Gaudí. Jujol collaborated with his maestro on the

View of Casa Vicens from the rear garden. A work by Gaudí's assistant, Francisco Berenguer Mestres, and by the painter Alejo Clapés Puig.

cathedral in Majorca and on Casa Milá, though his greatest contribution was at Park Güell—the decoration of the bench and vaulting of the hypostyle hall. The most outstanding examples of his work included the catenary arches, the wonderful furniture (including religious pieces), and the way in which he recycled elements of industrial waste and created beautiful interiors that were both subtle and colorful.

Gaudí's great strength, which has not been properly recognized until now, lay in the balance he struck between a respect for countless aspects of the Catalan craft tradition, and the innovations made available by industrialization. He had no intention of remaining stuck in medieval times, an approach advocated by the Romantics. Modernism was an attempt to create harmony between the work of the craftsman and industry—to mass-produce pieces but without losing any of the quality or "personality" of manual work, without surrendering to a depersonalized, repetitive, mechanized production. As an architect-craftsman, Gaudí took advantage of everything industry could offer, incorporating into his work the aspect that interested him. Unconventionally, however, he would take these industrial processes and subordinate them to the original handcrafted pieces he designed, and not the other way round. He was, therefore, a man of his time, who combined these two creative approaches to the greatest possible advantage. But the fusion of

Chimneys on the roof of Palace Güell formed out of intersections of simple geometric shapes, with conical pyramidal trunks, and all embellished with ceramic tiles.

different arts and techniques was not a feature of Gaudí's work alone—rather it is the manufacturing stamp of Modernism (and of all of its contemporary European manifestations), an attempt to enrich architecture and raise it to the level of a fine art that is complete and integrative.

Another important feature that is fundamental to this harmonious coexistence of traditional craftsmanship and industry, is the fact that Gaudí did not copy architectural styles from the past, a practice that was very common in his time. What he took from architectural tradition were the techniques and the basic elements, not the forms—just the spirit, as it were. He studied the achievements of the past but used them only as a starting point, never as the final objective. He took the same approach to the techniques of craftsmanship, never copying the forms, only the procedures, and in doing so he would improve them and introduce innovations, always going one step further, aided by industry. Moreover, in his capacity as craftsman-architect (that is to say, a craftsman of architecture) Gaudí never ceased his research into architecture, and his creations follow an evolutionary course that is continuous and inexorable. All of his works are masterpieces; at the same time they are experiments that he continually improved on and perfected. He made full use of each of his achievements, though without ever attempting to repeat any of them.

But what kind of craftsmen were available to Gaudí? Until the nineteenth century, the traditional Catalan craftsman worked in much the same way that his medieval forbears had, plying trades that were passed on from father to son, after the latter had undergone a rigorous apprenticeship (though never in the father's workshop) and submitted the pieces that he manufactured to a strict control. Craftsmen joined together in guilds and brotherhoods that were dedicated to patron saints, which gave them the right to be interred in urns or in the guild burial areas—such as the cloister in Barcelona cathedral—as well as the right of the widows and children of guild members to financial compensation on the death of the latter. Blacksmiths worked the iron using energy provided by the rivers, which turned the heavy hammers that beat the metal which had been heated in the furnace. "Forge" translates as *la fragua*—or *la Farga* in Catalan—and is a word which has given rise to a great many toponyms, the same as in Galician-Portuguese—*La Ferreira*. These forges were concentrated along the Pyrenees, particularly in the town of Ripoll, which was famous throughout Europe for its firearms, which were sold all over Spain.

Another example of handcrafted ironwork is the Romanesque grilles on the collegiate church of Cardona. Then there are the iron door fittings on many churches, and even noteworthy examples of liturgical fitments in iron, such as candelabras, censers, and crosses. The best of these in the Gothic style are the grilles on the cathedrals of Barcelona, Girona, Tarragona, and others, with their latches and typical "bunching" decorations, as well as some of the clocks in the bell towers. There was also armor, swords, and shields, which demonstrated the refined work of these craftsmen, who damascened pieces using fine metal inlaying, a technique inherited from the Arabs.

Another aspect to consider is that of boiler making. Gaudí's father had been a boilermaker, and by watching his father at work, the architect learned (as he said himself) the geometry of space. Beaten copper was especially used in the process of making all kinds of vessels for domestic use: pots, jugs, pans for making hot chocolate, and stills for distilling alcohol, and eau-de-vie from wine with a low alcohol content. Brass was also used, though to a lesser degree. Smelting was confined almost exclusively to bronze, which was used in the manufacture of bells and also, many years later, artillery pieces.

The manufacturing of ceramics was deeply rooted throughout Spain, a thousand-year-old tradition for making practical objects especially for cooking purposes but also for trade: for example, the amphorae that the Romans used to transport Spanish wine, wheat, and oil back to Italy. In fact, the amphorae cast during the era of Roman domination were of a particularly high quality (*terra sigillata*). During the Arabic period, glazing and metal highlighting were introduced, techniques that reached their zenith during the Gothic and Baroque periods, becoming particularly common during the latter. These techniques came from Italy, where they had originally arrived, curiously enough, from Catalonia. The Catalan origin of these ceramic techniques is perpetuated in "Maiolica," an Italian word that derives from Majorca. The process was not only used for floor surfaces, but also for skirting boards, wall surfaces, and even altar fronts. Two important elements from the Baroque period are the ceramic pieces decorated with pictures showing the different traditional trades of the time, and also the set square, which was widely used in architecture at the time.

Another technique that had been conserved was the use of blown glass for manufacturing objects, a technique dating back to Roman times. This technique limited the size of the pieces, however, as evidenced by the stained-glass windows in churches and the windows for houses, which were both made up of small pieces of leaded glass. It was not until the Industrial Revolution that it became possible to make large laminated glass surfaces, which in addition were free of the flaws that were inevitable in glass made by hand.

Until well into the twentieth century, Catalan builders continued to employ building techniques that went back to the pre-Romanesque era, and particularly to medieval times: Building *tapias*—walls made out of pressed earth—was a process used by the Iberians, as well as the Arabs; it is still used in Morocco and Yemen. To use *tapia* for the stables at Finca Güell, Gaudí hired builders from the town of Sucs (Lérida) who were still skilled in this technique. Although it was of Roman origin, the *tapia* technique was used in Catalonia in the early Middle Ages, with the first documented testimony dating back to 1407. The use of this "walled vaulting," which was also known as *maó de pla* (flat adobe), or Catalan style, eventually spread throughout the Mediterranean region.

As a substitute for the heavy stone vaulting of that time, very light, strong vaults or domes could be created that were two or more sheets (*or laminas latericias*) thick, by using a material that was cheap and that greatly simplified the construction process, rendering unnecessary complicated scaffolding, trusses, or large numbers of laborers. The most outstanding examples of construction using brickwork are the terrace roof of Casa Milá (with its ventilators, stairway exits, and chimneys), Casa Batlló, and Casa Bellesguard, as well as all the viaducts and containing walls at Park Güell and its famous bench, which was made—as was all the rest—of *latericio* pieces that were prefabricated and then assembled on-site.

With the exception only of Casa Milá, all of Gaudí's works could have been constructed by builders from Roman or medieval times, since no modern cranes were used, just simple wooden poles and scaffolding. Gaudí borrowed techniques from industry only for decorative arts or "lesser arts," not for construction purposes.

The Work of Gaudí's Craftsmen

As a result of Gaudí's knowledge and mastery of traditional craft techniques, and of the craftsmen's ability to adapt to his requests, needs, and ceaseless innovation, it became possible to create high-quality buildings that perfectly combined craftsmanship with industry.

Ceramics

Glazed ceramics, together with a preference for revealing the brickwork on the façades of buildings, is a *leitmotif* of Catalan Modernism, one that was recovered after the Great Exhibition of Barcelona in 1888. Gaudí, like many of his colleagues, custom-designed glazed ceramic tiles for some of his buildings: the exterior of Casa Vicens is dominated by ceramics, and the floor surface includes tiles that are decorated with different floral designs, as with the Capricho de Comillas (Santander). Before he baked and glazed some of the seriated pieces on the ridge that crowns the Park Güell bench, Jujol engraved Marian poetry on them, then arranged them on-site in an irregular pattern. The royal chapel in Palma cathedral was covered with local ceramics in the form of olive leaves and the coats of arms of Palma bishops, as was the vaulting in the Trinity chapel, though the decoration of the latter was never completed.

Casa Batlló includes a tower crowned with a bulbous top section and a four-armed cross, which was made all in one piece in Majorca, as well as the ceramic astragals on the façade. The other glazed ceramic tiles, which are decorated with beautiful color, were manufactured by Pujol and Bausis, a company in Esplugues de Llobregat, while the fish-scale-effect roof tiles were made by Sebastián Ribó. For the convex surfaces, the only way to apply glazed ceramic tiles was to cut them into sections first and then assemble them as a mosaic, piece by piece. Gaudí invented the simplest, most practical procedure (which was used for the first time at the Finca Güell); it involved placing a whole piece of glazed ceramic tile on a surface of newly laid cement and then breaking it with a hammer and arranging the resulting fragments in the space. This technique is called *trencadís* (from the Catalan, *trencar*, meaning "to break"). We can find examples of *trencadís* on the chimneys of the Palacio Güell, at Park Güell, and on the stairway exits and some of the chimneys at Casa Milá.

In addition, when Gaudí was constructing Park Güell, his friends gave him their broken plates, which he then applied, in a kind of ceramic collage, to the famous bench, and to the chimney of the building at the entrance, where the mushroom structure is formed out of red clay and the white spots are the bottoms of cups for hot chocolate. The park also includes vaulting soffits in the hypostyle hall, where Jujol combined ceramics with the bottoms of glass bottles, *porrones* (typical Catalan drinking vessels), and vinegar bottles.

Finally, for the Sagrada Familia, Gaudí used Murano glass on the decorations that crown the towers; the same material has also been used recently to decorate the vaulting of the central nave. This type of glass was specially chosen for its durability, because as these pieces are located high on the exterior of the structure and exposed to the elements, they would be very difficult to reach and extremely expensive—or even impossible—to replace.

All the Catalan Modernist architects designed flooring for the Escofet factory, which produced hydraulic mosaic floor surfaces, as seen in the firm's beautifully illustrated catalogs. The problem with this flooring was the limitation of the dimensions of the rooms in which the tiles were laid, and the large number of different pieces of which the patterns were comprised. Gaudí, however, designed a floor surface for Escofet that he had originally created for Casa Batlló, but which he finally installed at Casa Milá; it consisted of one single type of hexagonal floor tile, a shape that could be more easily adapted to any kind of floor, no matter how irregular they were in form. This also meant that when they were placed together with the six adjacent tiles, different marine motifs were created, such as octopuses, starfish, and sea snails. Using a single metal mold (which fortunately has been conserved to this day) it was possible to manufacture floor tiles that were relatively small but very strong as a result of their compact nature and the material of which they were made.

Palm leaf railings *(Chamaerops humilis)* around the garden of Casa Vicens. The leaves, which are made from cast iron, are secured onto a plate iron grid. The upper part and the lamppost (1927) are the work of the blacksmith Buenaventura Batlle.

Ironwork

Ironwork is an intrinsic feature in Gaudí's structures, and since he was the son of a smith he had been designing pieces in iron from the very beginning. Pieces such as the railings at Ciudadela Park and the street lamps in Plaza Real and Plaza de Palacio, which were prototypes of two different models to be used for public lighting in Barcelona, and which had been commissioned by the city council. The same body also commissioned a fountain that Gaudí designed for Plaza Catalunya, as well as some public urinals which were concealed by flower shops on the exterior, but which sadly never got beyond the planning stage.

All Gaudí's works contain a significant amount of ironwork, such as the eye-catching iron gate at Palacio Güell that screens the entrance from the street, and the highly original royal coat of arms of Aragon. Then there are the corbels that seem to be hanging but are in fact supporting the wooden ceilings, and the galleries that protect the building's counter-façade. Another striking feature is the weathervane that crowns the dome of the only central space of the palace, and which is made of pieces manufactured in Juan Oñós's workshop. In 1885 the same craftsmen produced a wrought-iron masterpiece: the famous entrance gate at Finca Güell, with its superb dragon with wings made out of interlaced metal rods. The gate swings on a vertical axis resting on a stonework pillar that is crowned with an orange tree with delicate antimony leaves. Another noteworthy feature of Finca Güell (though now it stands within the environs of the royal palace at Pedralbes) is the fountain, which has a wrought-iron spout in the shape of a dragon.

Then there are Casa Milá's highly original balconies, with rails made of wrought iron that was heated, beaten, and cooled. When the craftsmen began manufacturing these rails, Gaudí personally supervised their work at the workshops of Luís and José Badía (successors to Juan Oñós). After overseeing the work for seven hours, he finally told the ironworkers to go ahead and finish the rest in the same way. The ironwork frames of the main entrance doors, which contain pieces of glass that take their inspiration from tortoise shells, are particularly impressive.

For the railings at Casa Vicens, Gaudí designed the characteristic cast-iron palms by taking a terra-cotta mold of a real plant, to create another mold for casting the metal pieces. A particularly striking feature of Casa Batlló is the parapets on the balconies that are in the form of masks, and are also in cast iron. These were made using a life-size plaster model that Gaudí created himself, and which he used for making the molds for the aforementioned parapets.

And of course Gaudí's religious architecture was given just as much ironwork decoration. Wrought iron was used to make all the liturgical fittings for the crypt at the Sagrada Familia: the lectern, the candelabra for the Easter candle (with its marble base), the crucifix, the lamps for the chapels, as well as the grilles that enclose the large windows of the crypt's radial chapels. Note especially the railings covering the lower part of the mullion column on the central portal of the Birth of Christ façade, which includes a wire mesh that was produced by a machine expressly created for the job. Majorca Cathedral also contains a great deal of wrought ironwork: the lamps on the pillars, the sliding gate that closes off the high chapel, the stairway for lighting the altar candles, the lamp in the shape of a tiara, and the unfinished baldachin for the high altar. Last but not least, the gate at the entrance of the Escuelas Teresianas is absolutely magnificent.

Furniture from the entrance hall of La Pedrera, currently on the first floor of the Gaudí Museum-House in Park Güell. Includes benches, tall closets, doors and the dovetail jointing that surrounded the columns.

Wood

Wood also plays an important role in Gaudí's work: In one of his first projects, the Mataró Worker's Cooperative, he built wooden architectural catenary arches for the dyers' hall. The master carpenter who collaborated on most of Gaudí's buildings—working both on the structural carpentry and on the cabinetmaking—was Juan Munné, the same craftsman who had worked as a carpenter for the Güell and López families.

Wood also makes a significant appearance at Finca Güell, in the form of the magnificent rotunda galleries, as well as the shutters on the windows and the doors of the stables. The shutters on the window of the concierge's office have a decided Japanese influence. The beautiful ceilings at Palacio Güell are not just ornamental in purpose, they are also structural; they are not merely suspended from the beams of the wrought-iron sections, as is common, because the latter simply do not exist.

Casa Batlló has oak doors with air vents, splendid sash windows on the first floor, and wooden doors that separate the altar of the chapel from the dining room. There is a similar arrangement at Palacio Güell, where the main space was made into a chapel.

Stool from the first floor office at Casa Calvet, currently on show in the Gaudí Museum-House in Park Güell. Made of oak.

Gaudí often used the sliding doors manufactured by Eudaldo Puntí; when these doors were opened, the individual door leaves slid back into the wall. He installed these doors at Casa Vicens, Casa Batlló, Casa Milá, Palacio Güell, and at the house of the Marquess of Castelldosrius. As an indispensable accessory to his carpentry structures, the architect also designed ingenious bolts for the cupboards, such as the triangular ones at Casa Vicens, which lock both door leaves at the same time. There are also some spectacular gilded cast-brass door handles, whose unusual appearance is the result of squeezing a piece of clay with the hand, thereby obtaining a form that is completely natural, the best of all possible forms.

The wooden furniture designed by Gaudí is noteworthy not only for its beauty but also for its comfort, since the pieces are perfectly ergonomic. Their forms are not capricious, adhering only to functional criteria. He designed exclusive pieces of furniture for Casa Calvet, Casa Batlló, Casa Milá, and other houses, and he even designed his own desk (destroyed in 1936), which was manufactured by the Puntí company and included sculptures by Lorenzo Matamala.

Note also the liturgical fittings of the crypt at the Sagrada Familia: the presbytery benches, the movable pulpit, the confessionals, the sacristy cupboards with their iron decorations and folding doors, and the leaves of the rosary door in the cloister, which was destroyed in 1936 and later reproduced in 1939 by the Carpenters' Guild. All of these pieces were exquisitely crafted by Munné, as were the corresponding scale models. Other works of his include the carpentry at Astorga Episcopal Palace (1889)—or as much of it as he could complete prior to Gaudí's resignation in 1893—and the carpentry for Casa Botines in León (1892), in which the doors, supports, stairways, and partition walls represent mastery in carpentry. Between 1912 and 1917 Munné made the famous benches for the crypt at the Colonia Güell, all but twelve of which were destroyed in 1936. They were later reconstructed in 1956 by a carpenter named Gurb, based in the district of Gracia.

Armchair and table from the office on the first floor of Casa Calvet at no. 48, Calle Casp. Oak wood carved into organic forms by the cabinetmakers Casas & Bardés.

The dressing table of Isabel López Bru de Güell, from Güell palace on Calle Nou de la Rambla. It is now in the Gaudí Museum-House in Park Güell and is the property of the Güell family.

Grille on the front door of Casa Botines, in Leon; it was forged in the workshops of the Badia brothers, in Barcelona in 1892.

Other collaborators (though they only worked as cabinetmakers) included the master carpenters Casas and Bardés, journeymen employed at Eudaldo Puntí's workshop, who always worked for Gaudí. They were responsible for the furniture at Casa Calvet, Casa Batlló, and Casa Milá, while Munné did all the structural carpentry work. The door frames in Casa Batlló were highly innovative in that they were carved according to the natural grain of the tree trunk, an approach that made the final shape completely unpredictable. As Casa Milá was given a totally modern structure, comprised of metal pillars and beams and small brickwork vaults, the size and arrangement of the rooms could be changed. Originally this structure remained hidden by beautiful wattle screen and stucco ceilings, which were all different; Jujol collaborated on them, creating forms that were fantastic and poetic, even.

Another eye-catching feature is the remarkable entrance hall on the first floor of Casa Batlló, with its marine motifs, a fantastical built-in chimney, and the dining-room ceiling, which takes the form of a whirlpool with a lamp in the center.

The ceilings of Casa Vicens were very different, made of cardboard that was pressed and painted, then ornamented with remarkable plantlike decorations that seem to be made of plaster.

In addition to using traditional stained-glass sections, Gaudí created a brilliant system for the stained-glass windows of the cathedral at Palma de Majorca. Using natural light he direct mixed two sheets of glass colored in primary tones and one transparent sheet decorated with the grisaille. These, in turn, were protected externally by transparent sheets of glass. Gaudí's collaborators on this project were the artists Llongueras, Ivo Pascual, and Torres García, who did the graphic design for the windows.

We also have three examples of Gaudí reusing or recycling glass that had not been manufactured especially for the purpose: on the façade and chimneys of Casa Batlló, Gaudí used blue and pink pieces of glass that were given to him for free by a factory, since they were waste fragments produced by the laminating machines. Glass fragments were also used on the upper section of the Bellesguard tower to make the helicoidal heraldic coat of arms and the crown, in homage to Martín I of Aragon, the last monarch of the House of Barcelona. A final example is one of the chimneys on the roof terrace at Casa Milá (the one that was also plastered), which Gaudí decorated with the bottoms of champagne bottles.

Among all of the craftsmen who worked with Gaudí, there were a number of important artists, such as Lorenzo Matamala Piñol (1856–1927), who was a sculptor and one of Gaudí's great friends. Matamala first worked in Eudaldo Puntí's workshop, before later setting up his

Wattle screen and plaster ceiling in a room in Casa Milá. All the rooms were given different ceilings, which were built by the plasterers after Sugrañes and Canaleta had personally traced the shapes of the relief patterns.

1:10 scale models in plaster of the single and double chimneys on the roof of Casa Milá, constructed by Gaudí and his assistants in the basement of La Pedrera during its construction. Museum of Architecture of the *Real Catedra Gaudí*.

own business, and finally, in 1887, moving his entire team to work on the Sagrada Familia. He was responsible for the naturalistic sculpture on the capitals of the crypt, the animals on the buttresses of the apse, and the decorations crowning the pinnacles of same, which include plant motifs, all appearing just as they are in nature.

It was Gaudí who asked Matamala to come and work on the Sagrada Familia. They had been collaborating assiduously since 1878, creating pieces such as the architect's desk (manufactured in Puntí's workshop), the furnishings for the Pantheon at Comillas and the capitals for El Capricho in the same town, the lampposts in Plaza Real and various other pieces for Barcelona's Ciudadela Park. Another noteworthy example of his work is the figure of St. George on the front door of Casa Botines in León. Matamala later married the daughter of the sculptor Juan Flotats (who created the magnificent Annunciation relief that decorates the keystone of the vault in the central space of the crypt at the Sagrada Familia) and had a son, Juan Matamala Flotats (1893–1977), who also worked in close collaboration with Gaudí, above all on the Temple, and who would also become Gaudí's biographer.

Model Making

To create the angels for Majorca cathedral, Gaudí took photographs of models from many different positions, then worked with metal frameworks and structures which he subsequently covered in metal mesh. Gaudí also tried another innovative, totally hyper-realistic system of sculpture which involved taking molds directly from real people and animals; the results can be seen in the Birth of Christ façade on the Sagrada Familia. Gaudí decided to use this technique

1:10 scale model in plaster of one of the air vents on the roof of Casa Milá. Until 1970 they were in the possession of the builder who built the house, José Bayo Casanovas (1878-1970), since when they have been in the Museum of Architecture of the *Barcelona Real Catedra Gaudí.*

Balcony on the main floor of La Pedrera during construction (1909). The expressive power of these columns of Vilafranca stone is evident; they were worked using the point of a stonemason's hammer to achieve a strong texture that interplays with the light and shade.

for the façade because of the large number of statues needed for the piece; he had firmly rejected the idea of commissioning different teams of sculptors to create the figures, since this approach would be too costly. It was thanks to Matamala's team that the structure of the Sagrada Familia began to take shape, both on the exterior and the interior. The evolution of the interior can be seen in the four different structural models of the nave, some of which are quite large in size. These enabled Gaudí to continue improving the design without having to keep building sections that would later require alterations. This was, therefore, an economical way for Gaudí to experiment with the church's structure until he found the most satisfactory solution. The most outstanding of the original models (which were destroyed in 1936 and re-created at some time after 1939) was that of the Birth of Christ façade, which was built on a scale of 1:25 and then polychromed by Jujol. This model was shown at the 1910 Paris Exhibition. Some of the partial structural models were also impressive; for example, the 1:10 scale model of the naves (pillars, arches, and vaulting), and the models of the large windows and the roofing of the central nave. Construction of the model for the Gloria façade began in 1921, though this model was also destroyed later.

Access to the elevator at Casa Calvet. Columns of artificial granite, handrails and railings of wrought iron and plaster walls decorated with inscriptions that refer to the Poetic Floral Games, as well as motifs showing bunches of grapes.

Fragment of the Birth of Christ façade at the Sagrada Familia, with the inscription *Jesus, Mary,* and *Joseph,* and two angel trumpeters, the model for which was the draftsman Ricardo Opisso.

Of all the model makers who worked for Gaudí, it is worth mentioning Juan Bertran, an employee of the Matamala workshop. In 1898 he made a model of the façade of Casa Calvet and also collaborated on the model of Casa Batlló. It was Bertran who made the models of the chimneys and the exit stairways on the roof terrace at Casa Milá.

From 1909 on, the sculptor Carlos Mani Roig (1866–1911) was also one of Gaudí's collaborators; he created the stunning oratory crucifix at Casa Batlló (1907), as well as designing the image of the Virgin of the Rosary, which was to have been the central feature of the façade of Casa Milá, but which was the cause of a disagreement—though not of the definitive rupture—between the architect and his clients. At the request of the city council, Gaudí presented the plans for Casa Milá with an accompanying plaster model of the façade, and he also made models for the restoration of the Trinity Chapel in Palma de Majorca Cathedral and for the new tombs of Kings Jaime II and III of Majorca. The latter have since been lost.

But the star of all of Gaudí's models, which was not made of plaster, is undoubtedly the stereostatic model of the church at Colonia Güell, which disappeared in 1936 but has since been reconstructed. This model represented a brilliant revolution in modern building design methods, as it was made without recourse to any kind of calculation or drawing. The fact that it was never completed only adds to its attraction. Bertran worked together with the architects Canaleta and Berenguer to make this model.

Juan Munné's soffits and templates for Colonia Güell should also be recognized. He who made the molds for all the numerous prefabricated sections in Park Güell—the vaulting for the three viaducts and the nerves and small columns that decorate it—while his son and assistant, Agustín, made the famous washerwoman that decorates a buttress at the start of the portico just behind Eusebio Güell's house. Munné, Sr., also made the hexagonal molds for the bulging brickwork soffits, covered on the exterior with ceramics, that decorate the staircase, while the molds for the prefabricated decorative covering (made of small stones) on the façade of Casa Bellesguard are also attributed to him.

Rear facade of Casa Calvet in 1901, when the walls still decorated with different-colored engraved designs showing garlands, as well as the initials of the owner: PMC (Pedro Martir Calvet).

Casa Calvet

I will conclude with a brief analysis of the artistic techniques Gaudí used for Casa Calvet, a building of great merit that won the city council prize for the best building completed in 1899 (the first time the prize had been awarded). The house is a compendium of excellent all-around craftsmanship: In terms of construction, the most outstanding feature is the impeccable masonry, which consists of sandstone quarried on Montjuich, the same stone that was used for many of the city's medieval buildings. The main façade resembles a Baroque stone altarpiece, with boss bond ashlars that have a Roman touch, like those on the Tarragona aqueduct. Decorative sculpture abounds on the galleries, the prominent corbel-shaped balconies, the decoration of the façade with the two mixed-linear gables, and the busts of St. Ginés and St. Peter the Martyr, who were the patron saints of the owner—Pedro Mártir Calvet—and of the town of his birth—Vilassar. The balcony rails are also highly decorative.

Reinforced artificial stone was used for the Ionic columns in the entrance hall and for the Solomonic columns on the stairway, as well as for the opulent flowerpot holders on the counter-façade terrace, which were made by the firm Salvador Boadas.

In the interior of the building we find open brickwork vaulting on the stairways, which, as in all the contemporary buildings of Barcelona, are supported by only one wall, except on the landings. The design was drafted by the escaleristas (specialist stairway builders) who obtained the curve of the staircase by hanging a chain from its two ends and then inverting this form. And finally, the building includes an industrial construction feature: the lateral shop premises on the first floor feature large metal latticework beams. The flooring of the building consists of hydraulic mosaic from the Escofet firm—the famous company that provided most of the floors for the buildings of Barcelona during that period. Stucco decoration was used for the entrance hall and the stairwell, imitating the brickwork bond (and caligraphic combinations); in addition, as with many brickwork or masonry façades, imitation masonry quartering was applied. Stucco is also present in the relief decoration on the stairway arches, which includes polychromy. And, finally, stucco makes an appearance on the exterior—on the rear façade parapets, where it imitates a ceramic mosaic.

The use of ceramics is restricted to the supports in the main entrance hall, which are decorated with glazed ceramic tiles especially designed by Gaudí; these tiles, when combined with four blue-and-white floor tiles, create a pattern of spiral leaves. Wrought iron is used as an artistic complement in the form of an allegorical door knocker (a twisted iron cross that strikes a bedbug—an allegory of sin), which was manufactured by Juan Oñós, as well as the balcony rails on the main façade and the two splendid small balconies on the same side of the house, situated below the gables, with the fixed hoists for lifting furniture in and out of the house. There are also wrought-iron decorations at either end of the rails of the rear balconies. These balconies have artificial stone balustrades in the form of a convex latticework design. Note also the stairway grille, which takes the form of a band twisted into concentric circles; the elevator doors, which are a combination of wrought iron and cross-link mesh; and the lamp in the entrance hall.

Casa Calvet also contains some excellent examples of cabinetmaking, such as the doors for the main entrance, for the two shops, and for the entrance hall, as well as the front doors of the apartments. Wood is also used for the interior of the elevator, the stairway banisters, the benches in the entrance hall and those on each staircase landing, and the furniture in the apartments, which has been partially conserved. The blinds on both façades are also examples of cabinetmaking. It is said that, owing to a plasterers' strike and pressure of deadlines, Gaudí ordered the apartment ceilings to be decorated using carved wood with painted floral ornamentation.

The furniture designed for the office of the Calvet factory on the first floor is magnificent. The oak pieces were manufactured by the firm Casa & Bardés, and were joined without using any nails, just joints. These pieces were so strong that they withstood the blast from an anarchist's bomb on the Calle Caspe. Some of the sections of the pieces came apart in the explosion, but they did not break. Gilded cast brass, a metal so typical of Modernism, complements the cabinetry on the push-button control panel of the elevator, as well as on the handles and peepholes on the apartment doors. Gaudí created the shape of these handles manually from a lump of wet clay. In the main apartment, the door handle to the gallery (which leads to the patio) is an exception, as it is made of silver.

IN GAUDÍ'S OWN WORDS:
A COLLECTION OF WRITINGS

BIOGRAPHY

Maria Antonietta Crippa

Ornamentation

I propose to carry out some serious studies on Ornamentation.

My objective is to make it interesting and intelligible.

Ornamentation Makes Perfect

Examining photographs of the Alhambra, I have observed that the columns, as they are small in diameter, are shortened by lengthening the capital using wooden molds. I believe in the application of colors, especially on the base, in order to leave a short section of wood. The same with the different rooms: to support vaulting, small columns make the room seem bigger, playing games with the imagination, a little like Gothic canopies. The same with the bands that are superimposed: Their lines go in inverse directions. This is so that if the interior follows the pattern or motif lengthwise, the exterior follows the width; the latter is effected using Arabic inscriptions.

Subjects of Ornamentation

In order for it to be of interest, ornamentation must represent objects that evoke poetic ideas for us; these constitute motifs.

The motifs are historic, legendary, action-based, emblematic, and fantastic, concerned with man and his life, his actions and his passion. With respect to nature, they may depict animals, plants, topographical features, or minerals.

Conditions of Beauty

In order for an object to be extremely beautiful, its form should contain nothing superfluous, only the material properties that make it useful; bear in mind the material that is available and the purpose for which it is being applied, and all these factors will give rise to the general form. Consideration of the conservation of the object and of the material will give precision to the form of many of the parts, and the form of other parts may then be created from the contrast, that is, it will produce the most attractive form with which to make the neighboring sections much more attractive. And if, due to dynamics or atmospheric conditions, this approach does not produce satisfactory forms, then we will call in the assistance of purely ornamental motifs in order to complement the form, to help obscure its mechanical, material elements and to bring out the form that correctly satisfies the needs, circumstances that are determined by the object's "character."

Character

"Character" may be said to be the criterion for ornamentation. At present, character depends on the nationality of the person who is going to use the structure and on how it is to be used. A public structure must have a rather strict character, the very opposite of the character of a structure intended for a family or an individual.

A public structure must possess a character that is suitable for its use: gravity, greatness of form and simplicity. When enhancing the structure, one should not temper it with gentler designs that are naturally decipherable: Geometric designs that conserve the structure's distinction should be used, the former type of design being preferable for private structures.

Geometry

Geometry is extremely well suited to public and religious buildings; Greek temples and other buildings have a rectangular ground plan, conical columns, square metopes, and triangular pediments. As for ornamentation, there are countless variations that can decorate the individual sections, such as palmettes, which are no more than lines that are perpendicular to the horizontal line that they follow, and so on.

In cathedrals: the arch of the circle in the almost parabolic vaulting, the openwork, the combination of circles, the pyramids for the pinnacles and other spires, and the intertwining of geometric forms.

Large Masses

Large masses are always, in themselves, a feature of raised ornamentation. Consider, for example, the two-meter tambours that make up the columns of the Parthenon. What kind of ornamentation could be applied to these for the capital?. . . What better ornamentation than to make this grandness shine in all its purity? And what better approach than to create it, if possible, from profiles that are subtle but delicately energetic in certain sections, suggesting the strength and richness of the material and emphasizing the grandiosity?

Coloring

Ornamentation consists (as it always has and always will) of coloring, since nature does not produce any objects that are monotonously uniform. Everything in the plant world, in geology, in topography, and in the animal kingdom always has some kind of contrast in colors. Thus we are obliged to color, partially or completely, an architectural feature, and though this coloring may disappear, the hand of time will always provide it with another beautiful coloring of its own: that of antiquity.

Notes on the Family House (Casa Pairal)

The house is a little nation for the family.

The family, like a nation, has a history, connections with the exterior, changes of government, and so on.

The independent family possesses its own house—a privately owned house, that is to say, not a rented house.

The privately owned house is the country of one's birth; the rented house is the country of emigration. Thus the privately owned house is everyone's ideal.

The privately owned house can only be designed for a family, otherwise one is designing a rented house.

In the Catalan language, the family house has been given the name of *pairal* (family home). Who does not recall, on hearing this word, some beautiful example in the countryside or in the city? The pursuit of wealth and changes in customs have caused most of these family houses to disappear from the city; the ones that remain are in such a terrible state that they cannot last long.

The need for a family house is not only limited to one age and one family in particular; it is an enduring need for all families.

The independence of the dwelling, its correct orientation, and the abundance of air and light (usually lacking in urban dwellings) can be found in the infinite number of chalet-villas in the suburbs, in which most of the families will reside.

In order to find these qualities, inhabitants of the cities in other countries do not mind living outside the city center, though this is facilitated by the widespread public transport, which is fortunately now beginning to be developed in our cities.

And curiously, the rooms that are best equipped are those that are least used.

The point then, is, that we should make use of the resources that we have, that we should design a real dwelling for the family, and that by combining the urban dwelling and the chalet-villa, we create the *pairal* house. To do this, let us imagine a house that is neither large nor small, a house that we could call normal. By enhancement and enlarging, such a house is converted into a palace, and by reducing and economizing on materials and decorations it becomes a modest home for a well-off family.

Let us imagine a site in the Eixample district: large, in accordance with the owner's means, located in a neighborhood that may or may not be an aristocratic one (depending on the owner's fortune and position). It is surrounded by a wall that contains the garden and that is high enough to block views from the street. The wall is crowned with an openwork section (and on which young girls lean as they look out on the passers by at sunset). This roof terrace is interrupted by an arbor, next to the door. On the actual lot, on one side there is a long ramp, which is the carriage path. In front, there is a stairway from the top of which one can see the garden and, between the foliage of the poplars and of the plane trees, there is the house. The rooms are correctly oriented and laid out in a picturesque manner, as are the large bedroom windows. The study and the family living room are in the south section of the building, the winter dining room and drawing room in the west, while in the north there is the studio, the summer dining room, and the other rooms. Set apart from this group, but on the same side, are the kitchen and the auxiliary rooms. Between the bedroom and the study, shaded by acacias and laurels, there is a porch decorated with terra-cotta pieces, in which local sparrows nest. In the opposite corner there is a greenhouse made of iron and glass, a winter garden that adjoins with the drawing rooms and that can serve as a living room for big family parties. Throughout the whole interior one breathes simplicity as a system, good taste as a guide, and the satisfaction of needs and comforts as an obligation. Everything is formal. The interior is decorated with family souvenirs, the historic occasions, the vernacular legends, the delicate conceits of our poets, the scenes and spectacles of Mother Nature, all of which possess meaning and esteem. In short: from child down to child.

In summary, the house that we have imagined has two objectives: First, since it is a very hygienic structure, it ensures that the children who grow up under this roof are robust and healthy. Second, as a result of its artistic qualities, it will provide them, as far as possible, with our proverbial fullness of character. In short, it will make the children who are born there into true children of the *casa pairal*.

Reflections compiled by Gaudí's disciples between 1914 and 1926

The Spirit of Observation

One consequence of my weakness as a child was that I was often unable to take part in the games my friends were playing, and this helped to develop my sense of observation. Thus, once when the teacher told us that birds had wings so that they could fly, I replied: "The chickens on our farm have very big wings and they can't fly. They use them to help them run faster."

Mediterranean I

Virtue lies at the mid-point: *Mediterranean* means "between the land." On the coast of this ocean, where the medium-strength light falls at a 45-degree angle (which is the angle of light that best defines structures and brings out their form), great artistic cultures have flourished as a result of the balance of light: There is neither too much nor too little, because both extremes are blinding, and the blind cannot see. In the Mediterranean a specific view of things is established, the view that gives rise to true art. Our plastic strength is the balance between feelings and logic: The northern races are obsessed with suffocating feelings and this, together with the lack of light, produces phantoms, while those of the south, owing to an excess of light, neglect reality and create monsters. When light is insufficient or dazzling, people cannot see very well and their spirit is abstracted. The arts of the Mediterranean will always possess a marked superiority compared with those from the north, because they are derived from the observation of nature: The most that the poor Northerners can manage is to produce works that are attractive, but not perfect, and this is why they buy Mediterranean works. In turn, however, they are very gifted when it comes to analysis, science, and industry.

The Great Book of Nature I

The great book of nature is always open, and we should all make the effort to read it; other books are all derived from this one and include human mistakes and interpretations. There are two revelations: a doctrinaire one concerning morals and religion, and another one that is our guide to facts, and which is the great book of nature.

Airplanes are fitted with flat wings that cannot be folded up, just like insects, which for many centuries have been flying perfectly. The purpose of a building is to free us from the sun and the rain. A building is an imitation of the tree, a structure that absorbs both sun and rain. Our imitation stretches as far as the elements, as columns were first trees, and later we see capitals decorated with leaves. This is yet another justification for the Sagrada Familia.

The Great Book of Nature III

The tree near my workshop: *This* is my teacher!

Gardens

In our country there is a great variety of flowers and they are all perfumed; in the north flowers are few and they are not perfumed. There they suffer from a monotony of green which designers have to combat with curved, sinuous forms, while we do not suffer from monotony and can use rectangular forms. Curves are only justifiable in our country by irregularities in the terrain.

Our real gardens consist of flowers and shrubs (as we have few large trees, which in the north are very common), vegetables, almond trees, and fruit trees, while along the footpaths there are all kinds of flowers and vines within arm's reach.

The small city garden comprises a fountain with a path around it, a cross-path and a circular path, all filled with flowers.

Beauty II

Beauty is the brightness of Truth, and everyone is captivated by brightness, and this is why art attains such universality. In turn, science and reason are only for those with skilled minds.

Light

The essential quality for a work of art is harmony; plastic works are engendered by light, which decorates and creates relief. I suspect that the Latin word *decor* either means "light" or something closely connected with it, and which expresses clarity.

The light that creates the maximum harmony is the light that falls at a 45-degree angle, striking masses neither perpendicularly nor horizontally. This light, which is of medium-strength, gives the most perfect view of structures, and a more detailed perception. This light is the light of the Mediterranean—the people of the *Mediterranean* ("between the land") are the true repositories of plasticity; examples: Egypt, Greece, Italy. Architecture is, then, Mediterranean (the people of the North are more suited to science), because there is harmony of light, and this does not exist in the countries of the North, where the light is miserable and horizontal, nor in the hot countries, where it is vertical. Things cannot be seen very well in the poor light of the North or in the dazzling light of scorching climates. In both cases, people cannot see, and their spirit is abstracted. The Germans and the Hindus have both opted for a geometry that has no figures, which is the abstraction of abstraction.

The future is ours; the other Mediterranean countries are worn out and now is the moment for us to expand; we cannot deprive humanity of our creations.

The Arts

Architecture is the main plastic art; sculpture and painting both need this first art.

All of its excellence comes from light. Architecture is the organization of light, sculpture is playing with light, painting is the reproduction of light through color, which is the decomposition of light.

Originality III

Originality consists of returning to the origin; thus something is original when it returns, using the available resources, to the simplicity of the first architectural ideas. Thus it is original to design the extremely simple, primitive basilica using the complexity of the individual stability of the vaulting (as has been done in the Sagrada Familia).

Originality V

There is no need to desire to be original; everyone should learn from what has been done before, and, if they do not do so, they will not get anywhere and will make the same mistakes that have been made for centuries. The teachings of the past should not be looked down on. Everyone possesses his own style, and it emerges spontaneously without our realizing it.

My ideas stem from an indisputable logic. The only thing about them is that they have never been applied before, and the fact that I was the first one to use them is the only thing that leaves me feeling unsure about them.

Our Eyes

One day when I was having lunch with the Bishop of Majorca, someone spoke about how wonderful it was that images persisted in the retina, that magnificent photographic machine, and one of our fellow diners said that of course it was wonderful, because it is man's principal sense. I was surprised and, wishing to speak about this (it was one of those things that one thinks about sometimes), I said to him, "It is not the principal sense, as that is the sense of glory, because St. Peter says that glory is the vision of God—it is the sense of space, of plasticity, of light. The sense of hearing is not so perfect because it takes time. Vision is immensity—I can see what is there and what is not there.

Stability

Architecture is not stability. This is one part of it, but not all of it. An iron bridge is mechanical, but it is not attractive. Architecture is art; the mechanical part is the skeleton, the bone structure, but it needs the flesh that will give it harmony, or rather, the form that will cover it, and, once harmony has been obtained, we have art.

Order of Qualities

In architecture, form takes fourth place in order of importance: First is location; second is dimensions; third is material (color), and fourth is form. The sense of touch provides the form, but it does not locate it; the sense of sight locates the form and provides us with its color and its dimensions.

After these four comes stability, followed by the rest.

Color

The Greeks, whose temples were made of Pentelikon marble (a marble that is crystalline like sugar, transparent, and uncommonly beautiful) didn't think twice about painting on it, because color is life, and we should not denigrate this element, we should use it in our works.

The Architect II

The architect is also the foreman, the one who supervises the work, and as such he is a governor in the truest sense of the word. Because there are no official rules for how to proceed, he has to decide everything himself. Thus the great governors are called "builders of societies." That explains why, when the architect intervenes personally in the implementation of the plans, modifications are always made to them, to the extent that in order to possess the real plans for the structure, one would need to redraft them completely on completion of the building.

Le Corbusier

I saw a model made by this architect, and it consisted of a multitude of parallelepipeds. It looked like a freight platform at a station where boxes of packaging had been unloaded, with some of them resembling shelves: This man has the mentality of a carpenter.

Working within Classical Styles

When I had to build a structure within a specific traditional style, I tried to place myself inside the circumstances and characteristics of the style, and then I could create with freedom. It was with this approach that I made the colonnade Greek in Park Güell, Gothic at Casa Bellesguard and in Majorca, and baroque at Casa Calvet.

The Use of Curved Surfaces

The architectural styles that we might call cylinders are rigid, filled with inert masses for the purpose of stability, and are an obstacle to light.

Their rigidity and uniformity demands the use of strips, fluting, and moldings, which provide variety.

With the well-reasoned use of bulging surfaces, no moldings are needed; they are adaptable to all kinds of locations and volumes, by avoiding all laws concerning passive or inert masses, and producing, therefore, more light, where the light combines admirably with sound.

Architect and Engineer I

The architect is distinguished from the builder-engineer by the fact that the former effects the construction of the upper sections in a spiritual manner, or rather, these sections are for divine use. This also applies to houses or constructions to be used by human beings, as the latter structures must include a place dedicated to the worship of God in order for them to be complete. And this is not an idea invented by Christianity, as all pagan peoples had a place dedicated to the *lares* (Gods who protected the family). This is evident in the more than 2,000 figures in Campania museum, which were found in the *lares* halls.

Unlike some who adhere to archeological traditionalism and others who engage in arbitrary improvisation, I have followed a solidly reasoned, living traditionalism. Thus in the restoration of the Majorca cathedral, it is difficult to discern the authentic Gothic elements from the new ones that have been added, and where plateresque and baroque pieces have had their function changed and have been finished in a way that cannot be easily discovered. I made the archaic Doric colonnade in Park Güell in the same way that Greeks from a Mediterranean colony would have made it; the medieval country house Casa Bellesguard is as deeply Gothic as it is contemporary in style; and the apartment house in Calle Caspe is very much related to the Catalan baroque.

It is a question of placing yourself inside the time, the setting, and the resources available, and anchoring your spirit there.

Man's Dwelling

An apartment for a well-off person requires a surface area of 6,000 palms [one palm = 21 cm]; with a little ingenuity, this can be reduced to 5,000. Thus a house, in order to have two apartments on each level or floor, requires 12,000 palms.

A bedroom that is neither large nor small will be four by four meters; what is decreased in one dimension can be increased in the other.

The bathroom must be large, with space in which to dress, as well as a sink and a lavatory. It must be made so that one can walk around the bathtub.

A "cheap" construction (calculating the smallest possible dimensions) used to cost 4 *duros* [one duro = 2 cents] a palm; nowadays it costs more.

A decent set of stairs will be 1.25 meters wide; a comfortable passageway is 1.25 meters wide; in working-class houses they are made 1 meter wide.

Casa Milá is 48,000 palms in size and cost 400,000 *duros* (400 dollars). Casa Calvet cost 100,000 *duros* (100 dollars) and Casa Batlló (major renovation) 80,000 *duros* (90 dollars).

A bathroom must be spacious, with room to dress comfortably and with enough space so that, when a handicapped or paralyzed person has to be bathed, there is room for the two or three persons who will be helping to bathe him. It does not matter if it is adjacent and connected to the bedrooms, because it is also to be used by guests and by those who live in the house at other times apart from when they get up in the morning.

Nowadays the lavatory does not need direct ventilation, nor does it have to be located on the *galeria* (the rear balcony) or places separated from the main part of the house; with the advent of sewer piping it is has become a room like any other.

In houses without a great deal of space available, the toilet is located in the bathroom itself (another way of ensuring that it may be used by everyone at any time), because bathing stimulates the expulsion of urine and of fecal matter.

The dining room and the living room must be adjacent. The former is more important, as we often invite our friends to come and dine, and you cannot have a private party without food. The living room and dining room are separated by glazed sections, with two communicating doors, or one large one. In this way one can see from either of the two spaces into the other.

In houses nowadays, passageways, corridors, and staircases should be 1.20 or 1.25 meters in wide, while in working-class houses passageways will be 1 meter wide and staircases 0.9 or 1 meter wide.

The servants' bedroom often opens onto the staircase. All bedrooms need direct ventilation; an interior room should never be used as a bedroom.

Kitchens should be kept ventilated by a special airshaft, so that the smell of cooking does not spread up the staircase or into the rooms.

Supports and Supported Sections

The false distinction between supporting elements and supported sections results in an imperfect discontinuity between the upright, or column, and the arch, or lintel. Designers try to conceal this discontinuity using decorative elements: capitals, cartouches, and fascias, and so on. In the same way, medieval planners used ornamentation to hide false structural forms, a type of ornamentation that in general is not particularly visible, as they repeated the elements industrially without bearing in mind proportion or location.

Moldings

A molding is not complete until it has been decorated with leaf motifs, egg shapes, or waves, that is to say, until it no longer possesses its parabolic covering.

Thus if one uses ruled curved walls, moldings will not fit.

Rural Constructions

These should be built using materials from the actual site, and used in such as way that a farmer can build one himself when the pressures of farm work allow him to do so. The simplest, most effective, and prettiest type of enclosure is that of the bramble hedge, because it flowers and it loses its leaves—or rather, that it is one of the most varied of its kind.

The enclosing walls, the borders, the huts, and the little chalets should be made out of *tapia* (mud and dry stones), without the use of mortar. (If mortar is used the help of a builder is required, which is expensive.) Laying the stones without mortar means that there is no problem if one wishes to extend the structure and, therefore, balanced forms are adopted. And that is nothing new, since the stone towers of Majorca, the vineyard huts, and the borders are ancient.

Building on Mountains

Things should be left (without disturbing anything) completely asymmetrical: stepped buildings, unequal sections, and so on. Symmetry is appropriate for the flatland, and trying to impose it onto a mountain means the structure's qualities of adaptation and character are reduced, thereby obtaining an unexpressive coldness at a high price.

Park Güell I

When Dr. Torras i Bages came to see Park Güell while it was under construction, after walking around for a while with his head thrust forward a little, like a typical shortsighted person, he said: "I see, I see. You have made use of the topography to obtain the maximum comfort"—a fair comment, as he was a great bishop in all senses of the word. "Being physically shortsighted, he possessed an increased mental view."

Park Güell II

The objective is to increase and accommodate the communications between the different points of the park, using only the materials found on-site.

If the land had consisted of soil, a series of excavations and complementary embankments would have been made, but this would have involved pulling up expanses of rock, so it was deemed preferable to pull up *only* the stone necessary to construct a number of viaducts, rather than to excavate the terrain and build stone embankments.

Casa Vicens

When I went to take the measurements of the lot, it was completely covered with little yellow flowers, which I came to use as an ornamental subject in ceramics. I also found a lush palmetto, the leaves of which I transposed into cast iron and then covered the railings and the entrance gate of the house with them.

León

Because work could not continue during the winter, I began construction only after I had the stone for the façades all prepared and the structural elements all ready. The townspeople admired the speed with which the framing of that great hulking thing was assembled. As it snows heavily around here, I covered the house with a steep-sloped slate roof and gave the corner towers sharp, conical tops. I also purposely left stones projecting from the walls so that when snow fell it would build up on them. At the first snowfall, everyone came to watch the spectacle.

Casa Calvet

When the plasterers had to start on the ceilings, which were to be highly ornamented, they went on a strike, and so to avoid having to stop work (and to teach them a lesson) I decided to replace the plaster ceilings with simple coffered ceilings of no great thickness. This meant that I had to be very careful with the details in the spaces between the beams, which in the end were fluted, and I had to put some decoration on the frames to make them look bigger and echo the leaf moldings.

Casa Milá I

The patina of the stone, decorated with climbing plants and flowers on the balconies, would give a permanently varied coloring to the house.

Casa Milá II

The work was conceived as a monument to the *Virgen del Rosal* (the Virgin of the Rose Tree), seeing as Barcelona is lacking in monuments. And, since the cost would be very high, I had to be very sparing with respect to the construction: I built Casa Milà cheaply by selecting materials with high strength coefficients.

Casa Milá III

I would not be surprised if, in the future, this house were converted into a great hotel, given the facility with which the distributions can be changed and the abundance of bathrooms.

Casa Milá IV

My first idea was to build a double ramp around the largest courtyard area so that people could reach the apartments in carriages (we planned for a maximum gradient of 10 percent). This would necessitate a large ramp and, therefore, a large area (double the surface area occupied by the house). Second, one consequence would have been a need for large entrance halls and tall apartments. Thus a series of main dwellings level with the ground were built.

But even though this is the largest house that has been built, it was still not large enough for this idea to be developed. This always happens when building houses—contrary to what happens with churches, where things have to be made smaller and one has to keep the different architectural solutions to a minimum.

Geometry II

When creating surfaces, geometry does not complicate the construction process, it simplifies it. The most difficult thing to achieve is the algebraic expression of geometric shapes, which, as they cannot be fully expressed, give rise to misunderstandings. These misunderstandings can be made to disappear by marrying the shapes to the volumes within the space.

Perfection of Continuous Forms

Continuous forms are perfect forms. Normally an incorrect distinction is made between uprights and supported elements, since some are both uprights and supported sections. This distinction creates the imperfect point, which derives from the idea of continuity, since an element that is understood to be an upright becomes a supported element. In the spans, going from the uprights to the lintel, ornaments are placed (capitals, fascias, or cartouches) in order to distract the attention from a place that has not been well resolved in a mechanical sense. A conceptual deficiency is patched over with a visually attractive little detail, and the focus moves from the structural to the decorative.

Polyhedral forms and those erroneously called "geometric" are not commonly found in the natural world. Even the pieces that man makes flat (i.e. doors, tables, and boards) will all warp over time.

Stability and Form

The concept of stability and the concept of form are separate. When stability and form converge, they are actually parallel or they are divergent, depending.

Terrifying Projections

According to one of Gaudí's disciples: In Casa Vicens, Gaudí built a tower instead of a corner, which was supported by sheet arches made of beams in a rising projection. While the tower was under construction, one of the builders warned Gaudí that it would collapse. The architect told him to calm down, but when it was time to go home, the man, who was frightened, stood there waiting for what he believed was an imminent catastrophe. When Gaudí heard about this, he called over to the man and said to him: "You can only see the beams that are sticking out, you don't remember the ones that are inside!"

Reinforced Concrete

Reinforced construction is the most rational way of building, because all buildings are exposed to vibrations and movements that are hard to analyze (expansion, compression, and so on). All of this causes the structure to bend, and therefore reinforcement is the appropriate solution.

NOTE

The fragments transcribed below have been extracted from the volume by I. Puig-Boada, *El pensament de Gaudí:. Compilació de textos i comentaris*, published by the Catalonia College of Architects (Barcelona, 1981). An Italian edition of Gaudí's words also exists: A. Gaudí, *Idee per l'architettura—scritti e pensieri raccolti dagli allievi*, edited by M. A. Crippa, (Milan: Jaka Books, 1995).

For this book, the first, general sections have been taken from the Reus manuscript of 1878 on ornamentation and the short text entitled *Apunts sobre la casa familiar (pairal)*. From the second section, Reflections Compiled by Gaudí's Disciples, we have taken the following fragments: *On the Mediterranean:* L'esperit d'observació; Mediterrani I; El gran llibre de la Naturalesa I, El gran llibre de la Naturalesa III, Jardins. *On the arts:* Bellesa II; La llum; Les arts; Originalitat III; Originalitat V; Els ulls. *On architecture:* L'estabilitat; Ordre de qualitats; El color; L'arquitecte II; Le Corbusier; Treballar dintre estils clàssics; Us de les enguerxides; Arquitecte i enginyer I; Tradició i innovació; L'habitació humana; Sustentans i sustentats; Motllures; Construccions rurals; Construccions a muntanya; Parc Güell I; Parc Güell II; Casa Vicens; Lleó; Casa Calvet; Casa Milà I; Casa Milà II; Casa Milà III; Casa Milà IV. *On geometry:* Geometria II; Perfecció de les formes contínues. *On stability:* Estabilitat i forma; Els voladius esglaiadors; Formigó armat.

BIOGRAPHICAL NOTE

We know very few details concerning the life of Antonio Gaudí; we know a little more about his early and later years, while little is known about the intervening period, during which the most decisive events of his mature years as a man and as an architect took place. He was the son of Francesc Gaudí i Serra, a boilermaker, and Antònia Cornet i Bertran. Antoni Plàcid Guillem Gaudí i Cornet was born on 25th June 1852. He first went to school in the city of Reus, in the Tarragona region – an arid, stony land which was characterized by large expanses of olive and almond trees and vines.

His childhood was blighted by frequent attacks of rheumatic illnesses, which encouraged his innate capacity for observation and his love for nature. In 1868, having finished his primary and secondary studies at the Pías schools in Reus, he moved to Barcelona. It was here, in 1869, that he attended the preparatory courses in the Science Faculty so that he could enroll in the Higher School of Architecture, where he began his studies in 1873. He officially completed his studies on 15th March 1878. In 1876 his mother died, and then in 1879 his sister Rosita also passed away.

Though he was a student whose work was intermittent and inconsistent in quality, he was attracted very early on by the texts of the restoration architect and historian E. Viollet Le Duc and by those of John Ruskin, as well as by the classes in classical literature and aesthetics that were given as part of other university courses. Financial reasons led Gaudí to work (though still a student) in many of the studios of the famous architects of Barcelona.

From 1878 onwards he devoted himself entirely to his profession, initially working with the intensity of someone who wishes to involve himself in the cultural life of the country, and even to occupy a significant place within it. Then came his second stage, which followed a profound human and religious evolution, and produced in him a radical desire to serve, and a total distancing from any conventional form of relationship and public life. He had a passionate, impulsive, brusque temperament, and he was moody and prone to making paradoxical decisions; he was also gifted with an extraordinary imaginative capacity, and paid close attention to natural forms. Gaudí was passionately interested in all events concerned with Catalonia, his country, and though he never involved himself directly in politics, he was a fervent Catalan nationalist. He also paid close attention to the arguments of the workers' movements, he was often in the company of numerous important ecclesiastical personages who were in favor of the liturgical renovation that arose in Europe during those years, and his clients and patrons included personages of great prominence among the Catalan middle-classes. A decisive point in his life was when he met Eusebi Güell i Bacigalupi, who later became the first Count Güell.

Many sources record that after a brief period of intense participation in quotidian life, Gaudí changed his behavior and became elusive, solitary and totally indifferent to success. He spent almost the entire day at the site of the *Sagrada Familia*, where, as from 3rd November 1883, he was the master architect. He was also a frequent visitor to San Felipe Neri church, and was given to hard penitence (his Lent fast in 1894, almost cost him his life) and was completely indifferent to wealth. Perhaps it was because he had undergone a period of radical conversion, perhaps because he had developed certain ideas that had already been present in his youth, but the fact is that his life was characterized by "an exceptional dose of independence and a refusal to compromise to the canons of organized society" (R. Pane). His ecstasies of genius and his brusque personality did not prevent him from having numerous friends, even young people, while his collaborators from the last period of his life, considered him to be a good man, "with something close to a heroic saintliness" (C. Flores), and who was in spirit deeply affectionate and cordial.

In 1904 the City council awarded him first prize for the best modernist building in the city, *Casa Calvet*. In 1906 he moved, together with his niece and his father, to the house that he had designed in Park Güell, where he was soon left alone, since his father died in 1906 followed by his niece Rosa Egea in 1911. In 1910 an exhibition dedicated to him was held in the Gran Palais in Paris, organized by the "Societé nationale des Beaux Arts", on the prompting of G. Boucher, the director of the Salon D'Automme. This was the only one of its kind held outside Spain during his lifetime. He did not attend the exhibition, keeping to his deep-rooted habit of not traveling much. In 1922, the Spanish Architects' Congress was held in Barcelona, and was dedicated entirely to the works of Gaudí.

On 7th June he was run down by a tram while on his way to San Felipe Neri church, before going to the site of the *Sagrada Familia*. he died on 10th June in Santa Creu hospital. His funeral was held on 12th June, and during the course of it "an enormous crowd lined both sides of the street for four kilometers along the route of the funeral cortege. It was obvious that a great man had died." (G. Collins). In 1956, in the Higher School of Architecture, the *Cátedra Gaudí* (Gaudí Chair) was established, J.F. Ràfols i Fontanals being the first to hold this position. Gaudí's architecture is the object of growing interest to both critics and people all over the world.

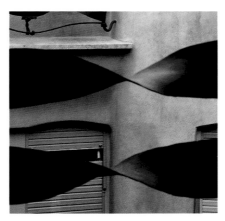

CASA MILÀ 1906-1910
Interior courtyard. Enlargement showing the windows.
Enlargement showing the wrought iron handrail.

Previous pages:
The interior from the exterior.
The exterior from the interior.

CASA MILÀ 1906-1910
Interior courtyard.
Enlargement showing a column.

CASA MILÀ. 1906-1910
Interior courtyard.
Enlargement showing a window.

CASA MILÀ. 1906-1910
Interior courtyard.
Enlargement showing
the covered stairway passage.

Following pages:
CASA BATLLÓ. 1904 -1906
Gallery of main apartment
looking onto the Paseo de Gracia

CASA MILÀ. 1906-1910
Interior façade. Enlargement.

Following pages:
Interior façade. Enlargement showing the handrail.
Interior façade. Enlargement.
Entrance from Calle Provença. Enlargement showing
the doorman's lodge.

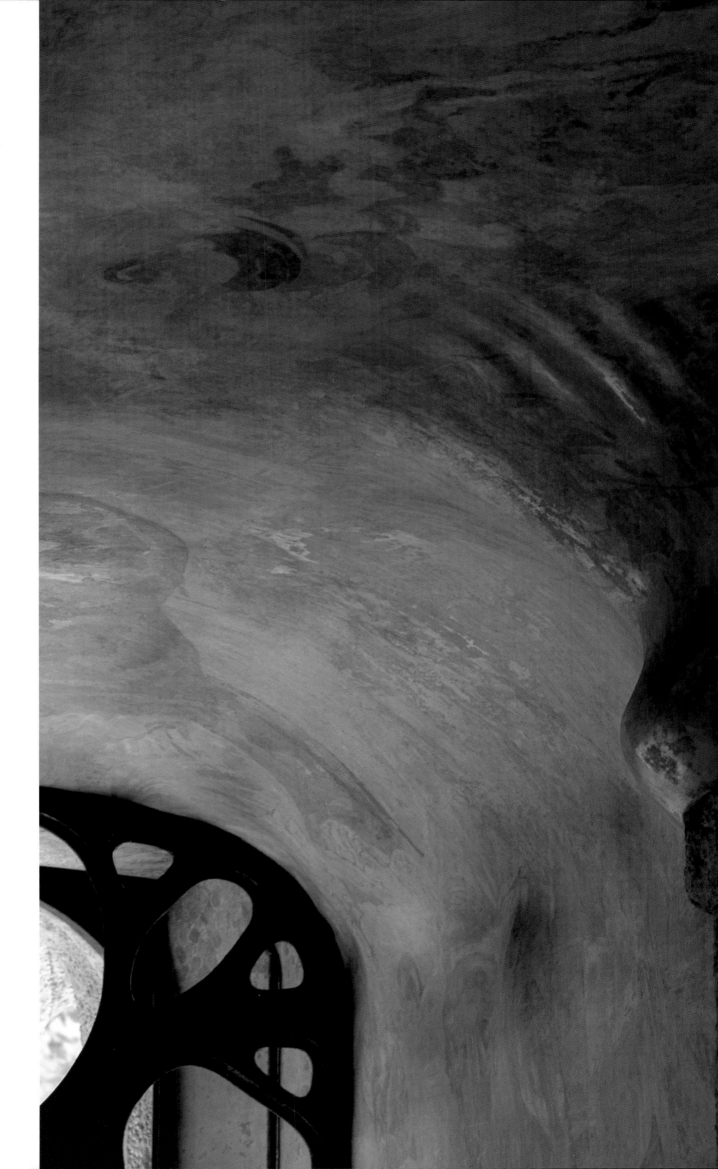

CASA MILÀ. 1906-1910
Interior courtyard.
Window. Interior courtyard.

Following page:
Interior façade. Enlargement.

CASA MILÀ. 1906-1910
Stone column in the main apartment.

Following pages:
Staircase to the main apartment. Enlargement.
Front door to the apartment.
Apartment corridor.

CASA BATLLÓ. 1904-1906
Fireplace of main apartment.
Interior door of main apartment.

129

CASA BATLLÓ. 1904-1906
Window above living room door.

Following page:
Doors of main living room.

PALACIO GÜELL. 1886-1888
Wood and wrought iron coffering
in the Hall. Enlargement.

Following page:
Second floor hall.

CASA MILÀ. 1906-1910
Structure of the attic. Enlargement showing the interior structure.

Following page:
PALACIO GÜELL. 1886-1888
Structure of the palace stables. Enlargement.

COLONIA GÜELL 1898-1914
Intrados of the stairway vaulting.

CASA MILÀ. 1906-1910
Catenary arches in the attic.

Following pages:
COLONIA GÜELL 1898-1914
Bench from the porch of the crypt.

PARK GÜELL. 1900-1914
Structure of the viaduct. Enlargement.

PALACIO GÜELL. 1886-1888
Dome of the hall.

Previous page:
PARK GÜELL. 1900-1914
Doric colonnade.

FINCA GÜELL. 1884
Interior dome of the coach house.

FINCA GÜELL. 1884
Interior structure of the stables.

CASA BATLLÒ. 1904-1906
Leaded window in the living room.

Following pages:
Sash windows in the living room.
Secondary stairway.

CASA BATLLÒ. 1904-1906
Courtyard area with ceramic tiling.

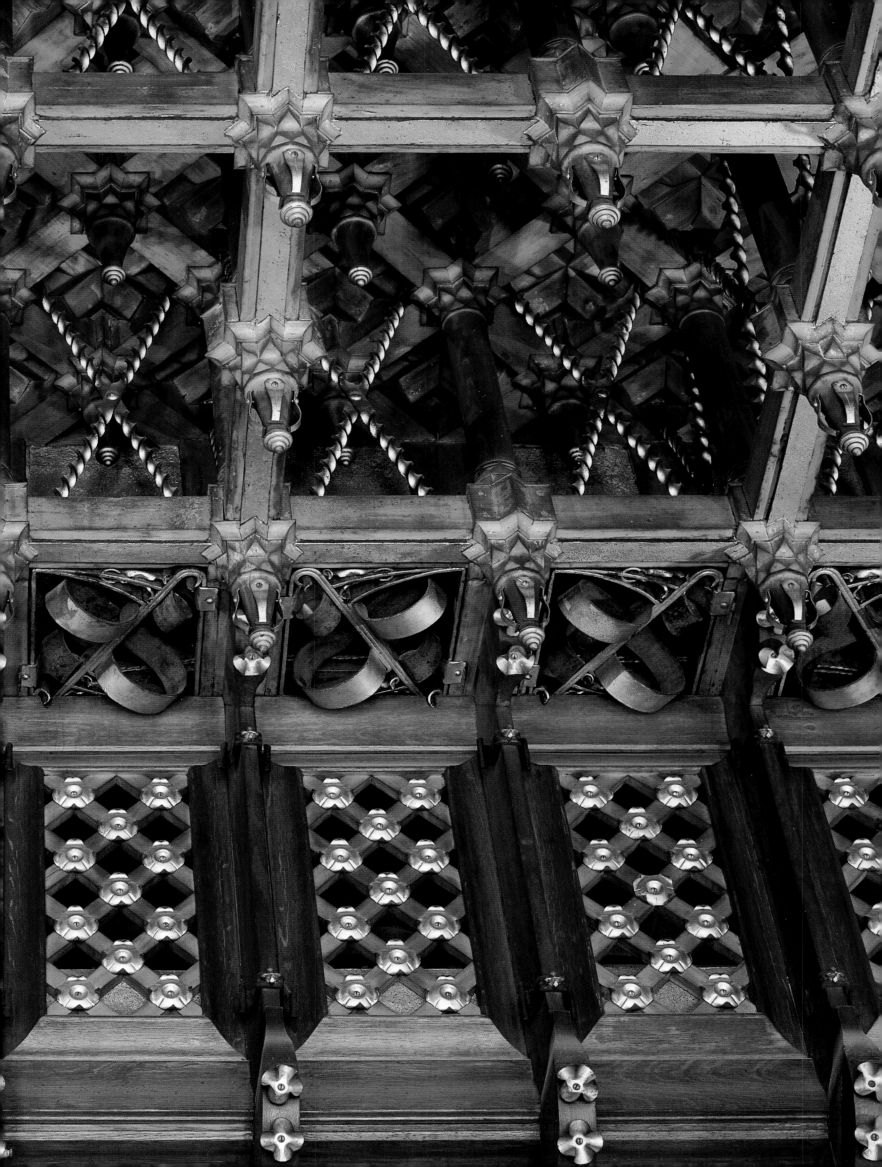

GÜELL PALACE. 1886-1888
Door and support in the waiting room.
Coffering in the entrance hall.

Previous pages:
Neo-Mudejar coffering in the waiting room. Enlargement.
Neo-Mudejar coffering in the tea room.

CRYPT AT THE SAGRADA FAMILIA
Ceremonial bench at the high altar.

CASA CALVET. 1898-1899
Bench. Front and rear view.

CASA CALVET. 1898-1899
Chair. Rear and side view.

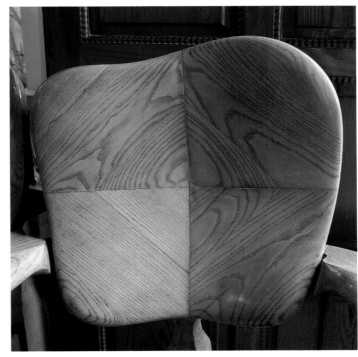

CASA CALVET. 1898-1899
Chair. Front view of backrest.
Chair. Rear view of backrest.
Easy chair. Front view of backrest.

CASA BATLLÓ. 1904-1906
Bench. Front view of backrest

CASA MILÀ. 1906-1910
Door. Enlargement showing a relief pattern.

Following page:
Parquet flooring in the living room.

CASA BATLLÓ. 1904-1906
Bench in the dining room of the Gaudí Museum-House
at Park Güell.

Following pages:
Easy chair from dining room.
CASA CALVET. 1898-1899
Easy chair from living room.

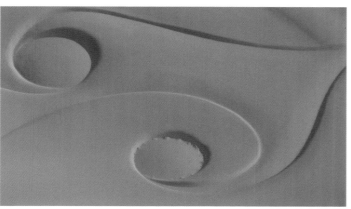

CASA MILÀ. 1906-1910
Plaster ceilings of the apartment.

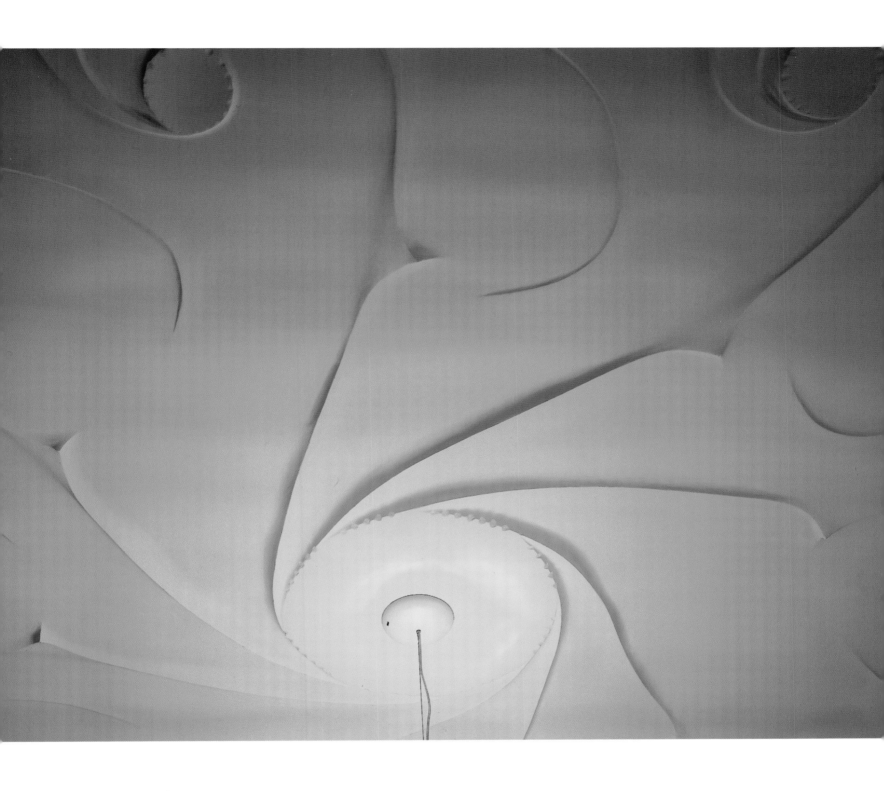

Previous pages:
CASA VICENS. 1883-1888
Look-out tower. Enlargement.

VILLA QUIJANO. 1883-1885
Look-out tower. Enlargement.

CASA BATLLÓ. 1904-1906
View of the roof.

PARK GÜELL. 1900-1914
Roof of the north pavilion.

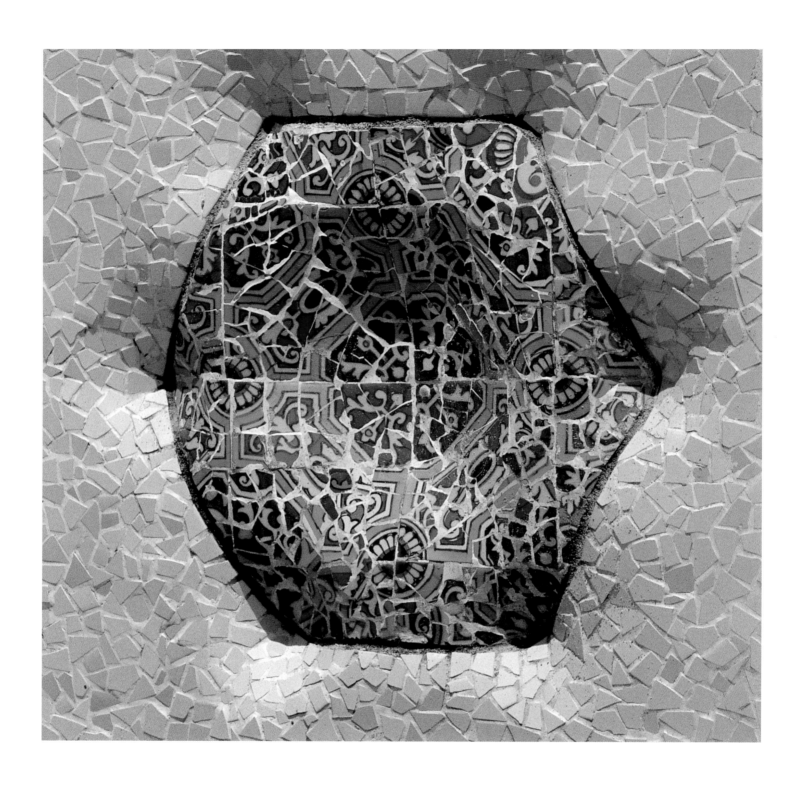

PARK GÜELL. 1900-1914
Examples of trencadis (broken glazed ceramic pieces).

PALACIO GÜELL. 1886-1888
Ventilation tower. Enlargement.

Following page:
PARK GÜELL. 1900-1914
Ventilation tower. Enlargement.

PARK GÜELL. 1900-1914
Trencadis on the wall and gallery of the north pavilion.

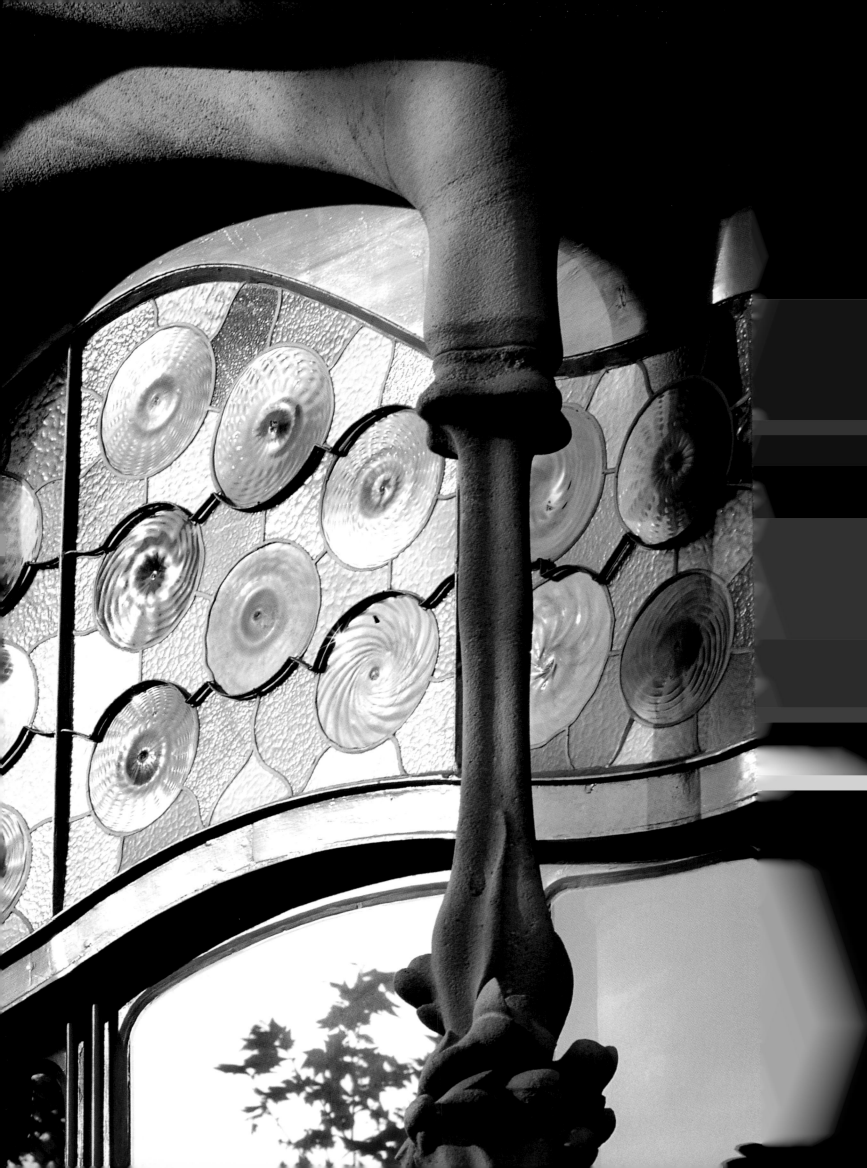

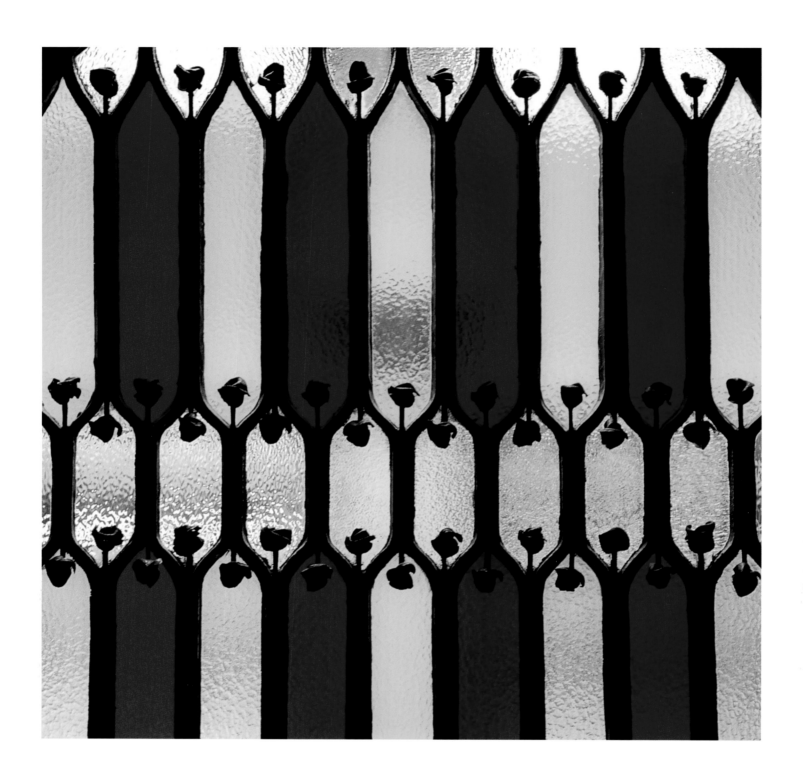

PALACIO GÜELL. 1886-1888
Glazed section in the entrance hall of the palace. Enlargement.

Previous pages:
CASA BATLLÓ. 1904-1906
Windows of main gallery.

CASA BELLESGUARD. 1900-1902
Glazed section on the stairway.

PALACIO GÜELL. 1886-1888
Carriage hall. Enlargement of the wrought iron section.

Following page:
Hall chapel. Enlargement showing the door.

FINCA GÜELL 1884
Wrought and cast iron entrance door.

Following page:
PALACIO GÜELL. 1886-1888
Coat of arms on the façade, a masterpiece of the locksmith's trade.

PALACIO GÜELL . 1886-1888
Coat of arms on the façade. Enlargement.
Grille on one of the palace entrance gates. Enlargement.

CASA VICENS. 1883-1888
Entrance hall grille. Enlargement.

PALACIO GÜELL. 1886-1888
Grille on one of the entrance gates, with the owner's initials.

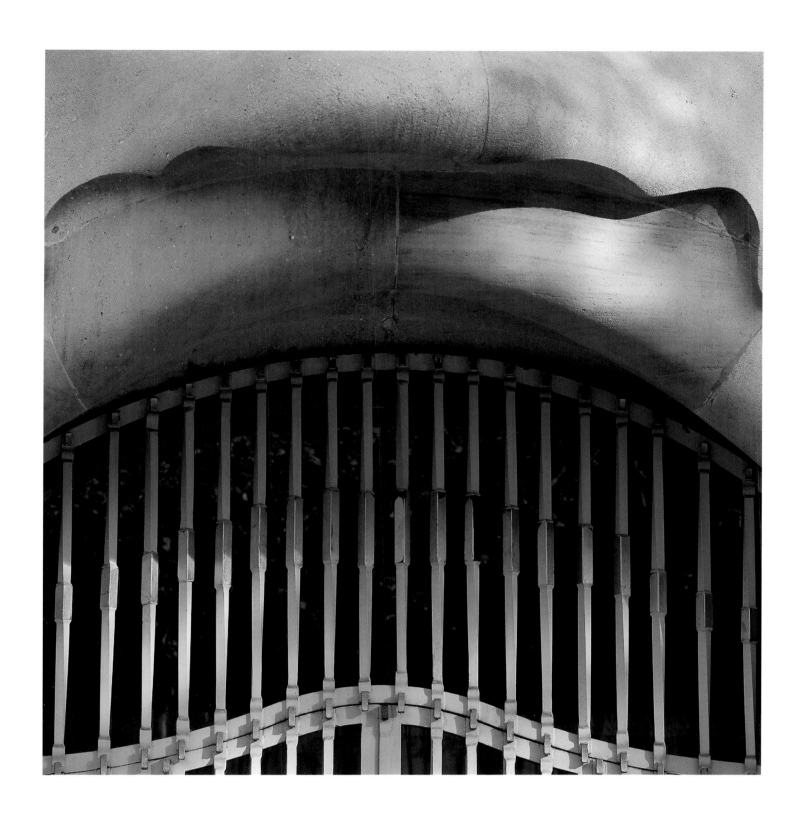

CASA BATLLÓ. 1904-1906
Grille on one of the entrance gates.

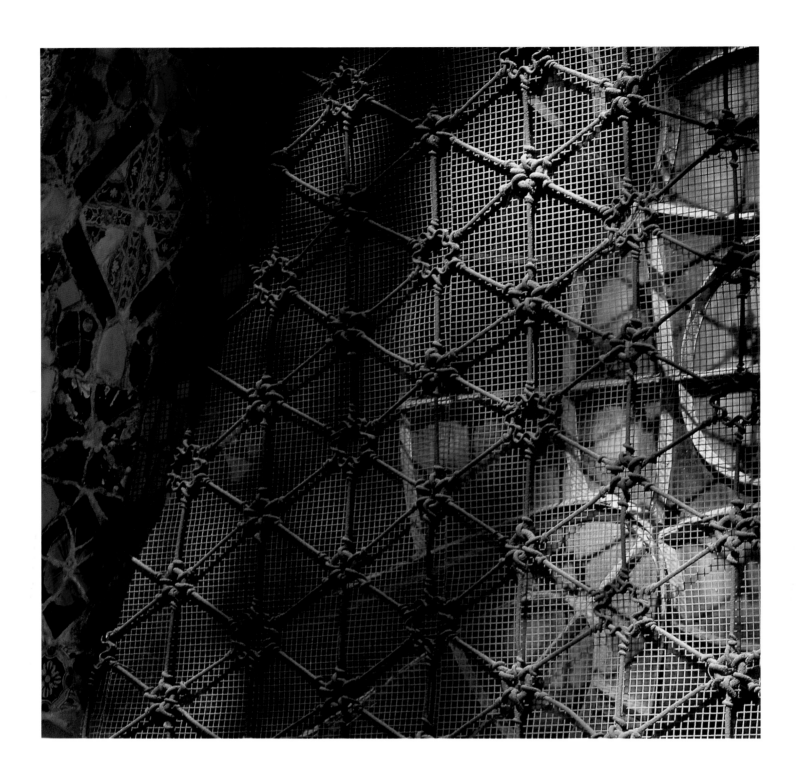

COLONIA GÜELL 1898-1914
Grille over one of the large windows in the crypt.

PARK GÜELL. 1900-1914
Wrought and cast iron door.

PARK GÜELL. 1900-1914
Grille on south pavilion.
Wrought and cast iron door.

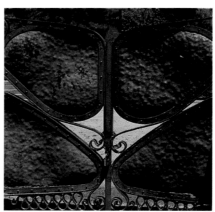

CASA MILÀ. 1906-1910
Façade. Enlargement showing the balcony handrails.

CASA BATLLÓ. 1904-1906
Façade. Enlargement showing the balcony handrails.

FINCA GÜELL. 1884
Door upright.
Wall of coach house.

FINCA GÜELL. 1884
Wall of gatekeeper's lodge.
Masonry of the handrails
on the roof of the gatekeeper's lodge.

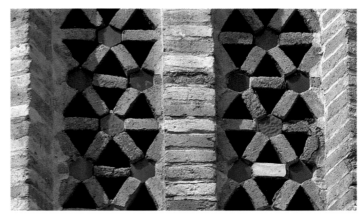

PALACIO GÜELL. 1886-1888
Façade gates.

CHURCH OF THE SAGRADA FAMILIA
Gable of the Birth of Christ façade
with the Crowning of the Virgin Mary.

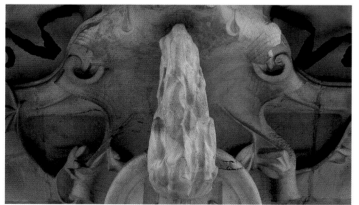

CASA CALVET 1898-1899
Gallery of main apartment. Enlargement.
The initials for "Calvet" and "Ciprés" on the front door.

CHURCH OF THE SAGRADA FAMILIA
Door of the Virgin of the Rose Tree. Interior of dome.
Interior of new dome awaiting sculpting.

Following pages:
CASA MILÀ. 1906-1910
Façade. Enlargement showing the windows.

CASA BATLLÓ. 1904-1906
Enlargement showing the entrance hall.

PARK GÜELL. 1900-1914
North pavilion.

Previous pages:
View of the entrance pavilions.
View of Gaudí's house.

PARK GÜELL. 1900-1914
Wall.

PARK GÜELL. 1900-1914
Roof of south pavilion.

PARK GÜELL. 1900-1914
Roof of north pavilion.

PARK GÜELL. 1900-1914
Entrance pavilion.
Window of south pavilion,
reflecting the four-armed cross.

Following pages:
Entrance pavilion.
Entrance steps.

PARK GÜELL. 1900-1914
Entrance steps. Enlargement showing the grotto-fountain.

PARK GÜELL. 1900-1914
The lizard-dragon on the stairway.

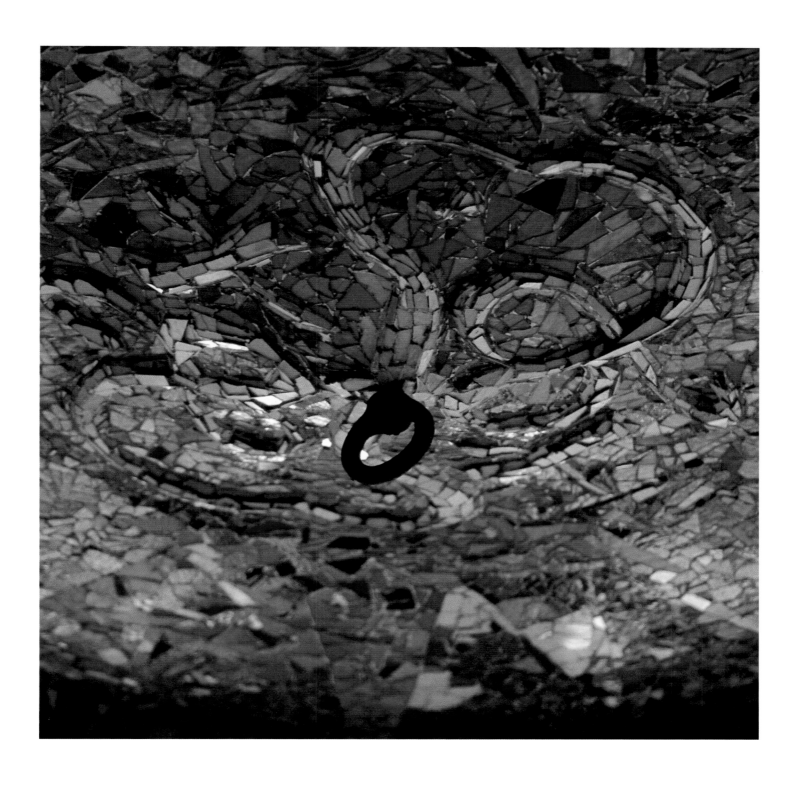

PARK GÜELL. 1900-1914
Soffit on the hypostyle hall ceiling, made by José M. Jujol.

PARK GÜELL. 1900-1914
Soffit on the ceiling of the hypostyle hall.

PARK GÜELL. 1900-1914
Viaduct interior.

Following pages:
Viaduct porch. Enlargement.

PARK GÜELL. 1900-1914
Viaduct interior.

Previous pages:
Viaduct porch. Enlargement.

PARK GÜELL. 1900-1914
Interior view of viaduct.
Following pages:
Exterior view of viaduct.

PARK GÜELL. 1900-1914
Benches – access path handrail.

PARK GÜELL. 1900-1914
Containing wall and access path handrail.

Following page:
Stairway at the Hill of the Mines (Hill of the Three Crosses).

SAMÀ PARK. 1881.
By the master builder Josep Fontserè.
Stone bridges in the garden.

SAMÀ PARK. 1881.
By the master builder Josep Fontserè.
Artificial cave-grotto.

PARK GÜELL. 1900-1914
Prickly pear in flower.

PARK GÜELL. 1900-1914
Carob tree and fruit.

PARK GÜELL. 1900-1914
Viaduct column. Enlargement.
Pine tree bark. Enlargement.

COLONIA GÜELL. 1898-1914
Porch column. Enlargement.
Palm tree bark. Enlargement.

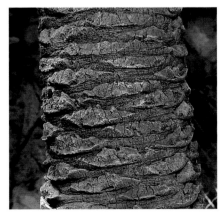

FINCA GÜELL. 1884-1887
Leaves of European fan palm.

CASA VICENS. 1883-1888
Door grille.

In the shelter of the Rock of Mont-roig.

CASA MILÀ. 1906-1910
Door moulding.

Following pages:
CHURCH OF THE SAGRADA FAMILIA
Birth of Christ façade. Door of Charity. Enlargement.

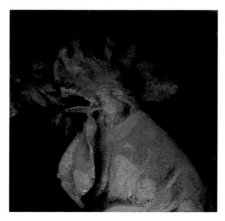

CHURCH OF THE SAGRADA FAMILIA
Birth of Christ façade. Door of Charity. *Lilium candidium.*
Birth of Christ façade. Door of Hope. Cockerel. Enlargement.

CHURCH OF THE SAGRADA FAMILIA
Birth of Christ façade. Door of Faith. *Nelumbo nucifera.*
Birth of Christ façade. Door of Charity. Turkey.

Following pages:
Birth of Christ façade. Door of Charity.
Enlargement showing birds.
Interior.

SELECTED BIBLIOGRAPHY*

AÑÓN, C.: *Jardines artísticos de España*, Espasa Calpe, Madrid, 1995.

«A + U» (Architecture and Urbanism), no. 86, Tokyo, 1977.

AWAZU, K.: *Gaudí*, Gendai Kikaku Sha, Tokyo, 1981.

BALBI, E. (ed.): *Gaudí*, Amigos de Gaudí-Uruguay, Montevideo, 1982.

BASSEGODA NONELL, J.: *Gaudí. Temas españoles*, Ministerio de Educación y Ciencia, Madrid, 1971.

– *Casa Milá, Casa Batlló, Colònia Güell*, Tres Uves, Barcelona, 1975.

– (ed.): *50 años de Gaudí*, Madrid, 1976.

– *La cerámica en la arquitectura de Gaudí*, Sevilla, 1978.

– *Gaudí, arte y arquitectura*, Rikuyosha Puplishing, Inc., Tokyo, 1985 (Japanese edition).

– «El arco de festón», in *Memorias de la Real Academia de Ciencias y Artes de Barcelona*, Barcelona, 1986.

– *El gran Gaudí*, Ausa, Sabadell, Barcelona, 1989.

– «Geometría reglada y arquitectura», in *Memorias de la Real Academia de Ciencias y Artes de Barcelona*, Barcelona, 1990.

– *Aproximación a Gaudí*, Cátedra Gaudí, Doce Calles, Madrid, 1992.

– *Jardines de Gaudí*, UPC, Barcelona, 2001.

BERGÓS, J.: «Les conferències de l'Ateneu: el cas Gaudí», in *Vida Lleidatana*, no. 14, Lérida, 1926.

– *Materiales y elementos de construcción*, Bosch, Barcelona, 1953 (in Catalan).

– *Gaudí*, Ministerio de Educación y Ciencia, Madrid, 1971.

– «Las conversaciones de Gaudí con J. Bergós Massó» (edited by J. Bassegoda Nonell), in *Temas de Arquitectura*, no. 112, Barcelona, 1974.

– *Antoni Gaudí: l'home i l'obra*, Ariel, Barcelona, 1954; *Gaudí, el hombre y la obra*, Universitat Politécnica, Barcelona, 1974; *Gaudí, el hombre y la obra*, Lunwerg, Barcelona, 2000 (in Spanish and Catalan).

BOHÍGAS, O.: *Arquitectura modernista*, Lumen, Barcelona, 1968 (second edition, 1973; third edition, 1983).

CASANELLES, E.: *Nueva visión de Gaudí*, Polígrafa, Barcelona, 1965 (English edition, 1968; Japanese edition, 1978).

CIRICI I PELLICER, A.: *El arte modernista catalán*, Aymà, Barcelona, 1951.

CIRLOT, J. E.: *El arte de Gaudí*, Omega, Barcelona, 1950.

CODINACHS: *Artículos, manuscritos, conversaciones y dibujos de Antonio Gaudí*, Colegio Oficial de Aparejadores, Murcia, 1982.

COLLINS, G. R.: *Antonio Gaudí*, G. Braziller, New York, 1960 (Italian edition, 1960; Spanish edition, 1961; German edition, 1962).

– «Antoni Gaudí. Structure and Form», in *Perspecta*, no. 8, Yale University, 1963.

– «The transfert of thin masonry vaulting from Spain to America», in *Journal of the Society of Architectural Historians*, XXVII, no. 3, 1968.

– FARINAS, M. E.: *Bibliography of Antonio Gaudí and the Catalan Movement, 1870-1930*, Papers of the American Association of Architectural Bibliographers, University Press of Virginia, Charlottesville, 1973.

– *The drawings of Antonio Gaudí*, The Drawing Center, New York, 1977 (Spanish edition, 1977).

– BASSEGODA NONELL, J.: *The desings and drawings of Antonio Gaudí*, Princeton Unversity Press, Princeton, 1983.

COLOMBIER, P. du: «Revanche de Gaudí», in *La Revue Française*, May, Paris, 1961.

CONILL, B.: «La serralleria d'en Gaudí», in *De l'art de la Forja*, no. 13, Barcelona, 1921.

CRIPPA, M. A. (ed.): *Gaudí e il sacro*, Tiarca, Bérgamo, 1988.

DALISI, R.: *Gaudí, mobili e oggetti*, Electa, Milan, 1979.

DESCHARNES, R.; PRÉVOST, C.: *La vision artistique et religieuse de Gaudí*, (intr. of S. Dalí), Edita, Lausanne, 1969 (second edition, 1982; in Catalan and Spanish, 1969; in English, 1971).

«Exposición Gaudí en Paris», in *Anuario de la Asociación de Arquitectos de Cataluña*, Barcelona, 1911.

«Exposición Gaudí en el Museum of Modern Art de New York», in *American Club*, Instituto de Estudios Norteamericanos, Barcelona, 1958.

FANTONE, C. R.: *Il mondo organico di Gaudí*, Alinea, Florence, 1999.

FLORES, C.: *Gaudí, Jujol y el modernismo catalán*, Aguilar, Madrid, 1982.

FLUVIÀ I ESCORSA, A. de: «Una familia catalana de industriales mecenas ennoblecidos: los Güell», in *Hidalguía*, Madrid, 1970.

FORESTIER: *Jardines*, Stylos, Barcelona, 1985.

Gaudí, Sogetsu Art Museum, Tokyo, 1978.

Gaudí, Finnish Museum of Architecture, Helsinki, 1981.

Gaudí (1852-1926), in Catalan, Musée des Beaux Arts Nîmes, Fundació Caixa de Pensions, Barcelona, 1986.

Gaudí, rationalist met perfecte materiaalbeheersing, Delft University Press, Delft, 1989.

GOMIS, J.; PRATS, J.: *Gaudí* (intr. of Le Corbusier), Polígrafa, Barcelona, 1967.

HITCHCOCK, H. R.: *Gaudí*, The Museum of Modern Art, New York, 1957.

IMAI, K.: «La moral del artista», in *Annual Journal of Tomon Architectural Society*, no. 2, Tokyo, 1958.

JOHNSON SWEENEY, J.; SERT, J. L.: *Gaudí*, F. A. Praeger Architectural Press, New York-London (Second edition, 1970); Il Saggiatore, Milan, 1961.

LACUESTA, R.; González, A.: *Arquitectura Modernista en Cataluña*, Gustavo Gili, Barcelona, 1990.

LAHUERTA, J. J.: *Antoni Gaudí 1852-1926. Architettura, ideologia politica*, Electa, Milan, 1994.

LE CORBUSIER, GOMIS, J.; PRATS VALLÉS, J.: *Gaudí: fotoscop*, R. M., Barcelona, 1958.

MARTINELL, C.: *Gaudinismo*, Amics de Gaudí, Barcelona, 1954.

MARTINELL BRUNET, C.: *Gaudí, su vida, su teoría, su obra*, Col·legi Oficial d'Arquitectes de Catalunya i Balears, Barcelona, 1967; *Gaudí, his life, his theories, his work*, Blume, Barcelona, 1975.

MARTORELL, J.: «Estructuras de ladrillo y hierro atirantado», in *Anuario de la Asociación de Arquitectos de Cataluña*, Barcelona, 1910.

MILÁ, E.: *El misterio Gaudí*, Martínez Roca, Barcelona, 1994.

Miscel·lània d'escrits de Antoni Gaudí: La seva vida, les seves obres, la seva mort, apareguts al volt del seu trapàs ara per primera vegada reunits en volum amb unes notes biogràfiques i il·lustracions, Políglota, Barcelona, 1926.

MOLEMA, J.: *Un camino hacia la originalidad*, Colegio de Arquitectos Técnicos, Barcelona, 1992.

MORAVANSKI, A.: *Antonio Gaudí*, Akademia Kiadò, Budapest, 1980.

MOWER, D.: *Gaudí*. Oresko Books, London, 1977.

NAVÉS VIÑAS, F.: *Càlcul d'estructures*, UPC, Barcelona, 1995.

– MENDOZA, M.: *Arquitectura del jardín y del paisaje*, Omega, Barcelona, 2001.

PANE, R.: *Antoni Gaudí*, Comunità, Milan, 1964 (Second edition, 1983).

PERUCHO, J.: *Gaudí, una arquitectura de anticipación*, Polígrafa, Barcelona, 1967.

PEVSNER, N.: «The strange architecture of A. Gaudí», in *Listener*, no. 7, 1952.

– «Gaudí. Pioneer or Outsider?», in *Architect's Journal*, no. 15, London, 1962.

PUIG BOADA, I.: *El pensament de Gaudí*, Col·legi d'Arquitectes de Catalunya, Barcelona, 1981; *Idee per l'achitettura* (edition of M. A. Crippa), Jaca Book, Milan, 1995.

PUJOL I BRULL, J.: «Arte e Industria», in *Arquitectura y Construcción*, no. 116, Barcelona, 1902.

RÀFOLS, J. F.: *Modernismo y Modernistas*, Destino, Barcelona, 1949 (in Spanish), (1982, in Catalan).

– FOLGUERA, F.: *Gaudí*, Canosa, Barcelona, 1929; (Aedos, Barcelona, 1952; 1960 in Catalan).

RIBAS PIERA, M.: «Consideraciones sobre Gaudí a través de sus obras urbanísticas», in *Cuaderns d'arquitectura y urbanisme*, no. 63, Barcelona, 1966.

– *Jardins de Catalunya*, Edicions 62, Barcelona, 1991.

ROVIRA RABASSA, A.: *Estereotomía de la piedra*, Librería y Estampería Artística, Barcelona, 1987.

RUBIÓ TUDURÍ, N.: *El problema de los espacios libres*, Ayuntamiento de Barcelona, Barcelona, 1926.

SOLÁ MORALES, I.: *J. Rubió i Bellver y la fortuna del gaudinismo*, COACB, Barcelona, 1975.

– *Gaudí*, Polígrafa, Barcelona, 1983.

– *Arquitectura modernista fin de siglo en Barcelona*, Gustavo Gili, Barcelona, 1992.

STEINER, G.: *Gaudí*, Dumond, Colonia, 1979.

TANAKA, S.: *Gaudí. Architectural works. Drawing of actual measurement*, Tokyo, 1987.

TARRAGÓ, S.: *Gaudí*, Escudo de Oro, Barcelona, 1985.

TESHIGAHARA, H.: «Gaudí», in *Japan Interior Desing*, no. 3, 1963.

TOMLOW, J.: *Das Modell*, Stuttgart, 1989.

TORII, T.: *El mundo enigmático de Gaudí*, Instituto de España, Madrid, 1983.

VINCA MASINI, L.: *Antonio Gaudí*, Sansoni, Florencia, 1969; (Spanish edition, 1970; English edition, 1970).

VV.AA.: *Antoni Gaudí*, Vallecchi, Florence, 1979.

– *Antoni Gaudí*, Serbal, Barcelona, 1991.

– *El árbol en jardinería y paisajismo*, Omega, Barcelona, 1992.

– *Antoni Gaudí. Una proposta di libertà*, Atas, Milan Polytechnic, Milan, 1994.

– *El paisaje y sus formas*, Omega, Barcelona, 2001.

ZERBST, R.: *Antoni Gaudí*, Taschen, Colonia, 1990.

ZEVI, B.: «Antoni Gaudí: il genio incompreso di Barcellona», in *Cronache di architettura*, vol. IV, Laterza, Bari, 1972.

– «Un genio catalano: A. Gaudí», in *Metron*, XXXVIII, 1980.

MONOGRAPHS

EL CAPRICHO

ARNÚS, M. M.: «El Capricho de Comillas», in *La Vanguardia*, 12 February 1985, Barcelona.

BASSEGODA NONELL, J.: «El Capricho de Comillas», in *La Vanguardia*, 17 February 1985, Barcelona.

HORNEDO, P.: *Miscelánea Comillas*, no. 47-48, 1967.

PESCADOR, M.: «Visita al Capricho», in *Alerta*, 24 August, Santander, 1986.

SÁNCHEZ TRUJILLANO, M. T.: *El Capricho*, vol. I, Altamira, Santander, 1975.

CASA VICENS

BASSEGODA NONELL, J.: «El proyecto de la Casa Vicens», in *La Vanguardia*, 8 March 1969, Barcelona.

– «Centenario de la Casa Vicens», in *La Vanguardia*, 14 August 1983, Barcelona.

PALACIO GÜELL

GONZÁLEZ, A.; CARBÓ, P.: «La azotea fantástica (la cubierta del Palau Güell)», in *Informes de la Construcción*, no. 408, 1990.

– MORENO, J.: «El Palau Güell de Barcelona. La construcción de una idea espacial», in *Informes de la Construcción*, no. 408, 1989.

PUIG BOADA, I.: «El Palacio Güell de la calle Conde del Asalto de Barcelona», in *Cuadernos de Arquitectura*, November 1944, Barcelona.

VV.AA.: *El Palau Güell*, Diputación de Barcelona, Barcelona, 1990.

BODEGAS GÜELL

SPEIDEL, M.: «Bodegas Güell in Garraf (1895–1901)», «*A + U*», July 1990.

CASA CALVET

DE VIGNOLA, J.: «La casa de los Sres. Calvet», in *Hispania*, no. 68, Barcelona, 1901

ASTORGA EPISCOPAL PALACE

ALONSO GAVELA, M. J.: *Gaudí en Astorga*, Instituto Fray Bernardino de Sahagún, León, 1971.

ALONSO LUENGO, L.: *Gaudí en Astorga*, Sierra, Astorga, 1952.

QUINTANA, C.: *El Palacio de Gaudí*, Astorga, 1972.

RIVERA BLANCO, J.: *El Palacio Episcopal de Gaudí y el «Museo de los Caminos» de Astorga*, Museo de los Caminos, Astorga, 1985.

CASA DE LOS BOTINES

MARTINELL, C.: «Gaudí en Astorga y León», in *Destino*, 2 October 1960, Barcelona.

CASA MILÀ

BASSEGODA NONELL, J.: *La Pedrera de Gaudí*, Caixa d'Estalvis de Catalunya, Barcelona, 1987.

– *La Pedrera de Gaudí*, Caixa de Catalunya, Barcelona, 1989.

CARANDELL, J. M.: *La Pedrera, cosmos de Gaudí*, Caixa de Catalunya, Barcelona, 1992.

CASANELLES, E.: «El cincuentenario de la Pedrera», in *Destino*, 18 March 1961, Barcelona.

GIRALT MIRACLE, D. (ed.): *La Pedrera - Arquitectura i història*, Caixa de Catalunya, Barcelona, 1999.

TAPIE, M.: *La Pedrera*, Polígrafa, Barcelona, 1973.

VILA RODRÍGUEZ, R.: «El uso del hierro en la Casa Milà «La Pedrera"», in *Informes de la construcción*, no. 408, Barcelona, 1991.

– «Il restauro della facciata di Casa Milá «La Pedrera", in *Frames*, no. 28, Faenza, 1992.

PARK GÜELL

BASSEGODA NONELL, J.: «El jardín de las Hespérides», in *Boletín de la Real Academia de San Fernando*, 1.º sem. 1978, Madrid.

– «L'ordre dóric del Parc Güell», in *Temple*, Barcelona, 1994.

– «El turò de les tres creus», in *Temple*, Barcelona, 1995.

– «Parc Güell, mitologia i nacionalisme», in *Reial Académia Catalana de Belles Arts de Sant Jordi*, Barcelona, 1997.

CASANELLA, E.: «El parque Güell. Barcelona ciudad de Gaudí», in *Destino*, 24 December 1960, Barcelona.

CIRLOT, L.: «Las ciudades jardines de España. Barcelona: el Parque Güell», in *Civitas*, no. 1, Barcelona, 1914.

GABANCHO, P.: *Guia El Parc Güell*, Ajuntament de Barcelona-Parcs i Jardins, Barcelona, 1998.

JOEDICKE, J.: «Antonio Gaudí», in *L'architecture d'aujourd'hui*, no. 33, 1962.

KENT, V.: *Hacia la arquitectura de un paraíso, Parc Güell*, Blume, Barcelona, 1993.

LLOPIS, A.: «La casa de Gaudí del Parque Güell», in *Destino*, 14 March 1962, Barcelona.

MARJANEDAS, A.: *El Parc Güell*, Ajuntament de Barcelona-Parcs i Jardins, Barcelona, 1986.

ROJO, E.: *Antonio Gaudí, ese desconocido: el Parc Güell*, Los Libros de la Frontera, Sant Cugat, 1987.

ROVIRA I PEI, J.: «Aspectos constructivos puestos de manifiesto en la restauración del Parc Güell de Barcelona», in *Informes de Construcción*, no. 408, 1990.

* The bibliography for Antonio Gaudí is enormous. What follows is a selection of the main texts, in chronological order, particularly those that address his houses, parks, and gardens. Where possible, the original edition is listed first, followed by the year and the language in which successive editions were printed.

INDEX